my **revisi⏻n** notes

KT-143-766

AQA GCSE (9–1) PE

PE

Second Edition

Kirk Bizley

HODDER EDUCATION
AN HACHETTE UK COMPANY

Once again, my thanks go out to my ever patient, loving wife Louise – I couldn't write anything without your support and understanding. Definitely my best friend, my constant and soul mate!

The Publishers would like to thank the following for permission to reproduce copyright material.

Photo credits: p10*l* sportgraphic/123RF.com; **p10***r* rihardzz/123RF.com; **p12** speedpix/Alamy Stock Photo; **p20** huaxiadragon/Fotolia; **p23***m* racorn/Shutterstock.com; **p23***bl* Rido/Shutterstock.com; **p23***bm* Daxiao Productions/Shutterstock.com; **p23***br* James Steidl/Shutterstock.com; **p31** Alessandro Zappalorto/Alamy Stock Photo; **p35** Pal Szilagyi Palko/Alamy Stock Photo; **p40** dpa picture alliance archive/Alamy Stock Photo; **p48** COO7/Shutterstock.com; **p51** CP DC Press/Shutterstock.com; **p57** Trevor Smith/Alamy Stock Photo; **p61** Wessel du Plooy/Shutterstock.com; **p64** Scott Hortop Images/Alamy Stock Photo; **p67** Severin Schweiger/Cultura/Getty Images; **p71** Food Standards Agency/Crown Copyright/Open Government Licence.

Every effort has been made to trace all copyright holders, but if any have been inadvertently overlooked, the Publishers will be pleased to make the necessary arrangements at the first opportunity.

Although every effort has been made to ensure that website addresses are correct at time of going to press, Hodder Education cannot be held responsible for the content of any website mentioned in this book. It is sometimes possible to find a relocated web page by typing in the address of the home page for a website in the URL window of your browser.

Hachette UK's policy is to use papers that are natural, renewable and recyclable products and made from wood grown in sustainable forests. The logging and manufacturing processes are expected to conform to the environmental regulations of the country of origin.

Orders: please contact Bookpoint Ltd, 130 Milton Park, Abingdon, Oxon OX14 4SE. Telephone: +44 (0)1235 827720. Fax: +44 (0)1235 400454. Email education@bookpoint.co.uk Lines are open from 9 a.m. to 5 p.m., Monday to Saturday, with a 24-hour message answering service. You can also order through our website: www.hoddereducation.co.uk

ISBN: 978 1 5104 0523 3

© Kirk Bizley

Second edition © 2017 Kirk Bizley
First published in 2014 by
Hodder Education
An Hachette UK Company
Carmelite House, 50 Victoria Embankment
London EC4Y 0DZ

www.hoddereducation.co.uk

Impression number   10 9 8 7 6 5 4
Year   2021 2020 2019 2018

All rights reserved. Apart from any use permitted under UK copyright law, no part of this publication may be reproduced or transmitted in any form or by any means, electronic or mechanical, including photocopying and recording, or held within any information storage and retrieval system, without permission in writing from the publisher or under licence from the Copyright Licensing Agency Limited. Further details of such licences (for reprographic reproduction) may be obtained from the Copyright Licensing Agency Limited, Saffron House, 6–10 Kirby Street, London EC1N 8TS.

Cover photo © Shutterstock/Tungphoto
Produced and typeset in Bembo by Gray Publishing, Tunbridge Wells, Kent
Printed in Spain

A catalogue record for this title is available from the British Library.

Get the most from this book

Everyone has to decide his or her own revision strategy, but it is essential to review your work, learn it and test your understanding. These Revision Notes will help you to do that in a planned way, topic by topic. Use this book as the cornerstone of your revision and don't hesitate to write in it — personalise your notes and check your progress by ticking off each section as you revise.

Tick to track your progress

Use the revision planner on pages iv and v to plan your revision, topic by topic. Tick each box when you have:

- revised and understood a topic
- tested yourself
- gone online to complete the quick quizzes.

You can also keep track of your revision by ticking off each topic heading in the book. You may find it helpful to add your own notes as you work through each topic.

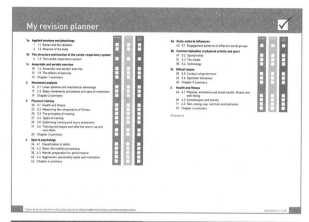

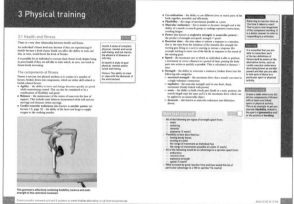

Features to help you succeed

Exam tips

Expert tips are given throughout the book to help you polish your exam technique in order to maximise your chances in the exam.

Typical mistakes

The author identifies the typical mistakes candidates make and explains how you can avoid them.

Now test yourself

These short, knowledge-based questions provide the first step in testing your learning. Answers are at the back of the book.

Definitions and key words

Clear, concise definitions of essential key terms are provided where they first appear.

Key words from the specification are highlighted in bold throughout the book.

Revision activities

These activities will help you to understand each topic in an interactive way.

Debates

Debates are highlighted to help you assess arguments and use evidence appropriately.

Summaries

The summaries provide a quick-check bullet list for each topic.

Online

Go online to try out the extra quick quizzes at **www.hoddereducation.co.uk/myrevisionnotes**

My revision planner

Countdown to my exams

6–8 weeks to go

- Start by looking at the specification — make sure you know exactly what material you need to revise and the style of the examination. Use the revision planner on pages 4 and 5 to familiarise yourself with the topics.
- Organise your notes, making sure you have covered everything on the specification. The revision planner will help you to group your notes into topics for the two separate exam papers.
- Work out a realistic revision plan that will allow you time for relaxation. Set aside days and times for all the subjects that you need to study, and stick to your timetable.
- Set yourself sensible targets. Break your revision down into focused sessions of around 40 minutes, divided by breaks. These Revision Notes organise the basic facts into short, memorable sections to make revising easier.

REVISED ☐

2–6 weeks to go

- Read through the relevant sections of this book and refer to the exam tips, exam summaries, typical mistakes and key terms. Tick off the topics as you feel confident about them. Highlight those topics you find difficult and look at them again in detail.
- Test your understanding of each topic by working through the 'Now test yourself' questions in the book. Look up the answers at the back of the book.
- Make a note of any problem areas as you revise, and ask your teacher to go over these in class.
- Look at past papers. They are one of the best ways to revise and practise your exam skills. Try out the extra quick quizzes at **www.therevisionbutton.co.uk/ myrevisionnotes**
- Use the revision activities to try out different revision methods. For example, you can make notes using mind maps, spider diagrams or flash cards.
- Track your progress using the revision planner and give yourself a reward when you have achieved your target.

REVISED ☐

One week to go

- Try to fit in at least one more timed practice of an entire past paper and seek feedback from your teacher, comparing your work closely with the mark scheme.
- Check the revision planner to make sure you haven't missed out any topics. Brush up on any areas of difficulty by talking them over with a friend or getting help from your teacher.
- Attend any revision classes put on by your teacher. Remember, he or she is an expert at preparing people for examinations.

REVISED ☐

The day before the examination

- Flick through these Revision Notes for useful reminders, for example the exam tips, exam summaries, typical mistakes and key terms.
- Check the time and place of your examination.
- Make sure you have everything you need — extra pens and pencils, a calculator, tissues, a watch, bottled water, sweets.
- Allow some time to relax and have an early night to ensure you are fresh and alert for the examinations.

REVISED ☐

My exams

PE Paper 1

Date: 13 May 2020

Time: ....

Location: school

PE Paper 2

Date: 15th May 2020

Time: ....

Location: school

1a Applied anatomy and physiology

1.1 Bones and the skeleton

Functions of the skeleton

The skeleton primarily provides a framework for movement (this is in conjunction with the muscular system, see Section 1.2, page 4) but it also has the following functions:

- **Support** – the muscles and vital organs (such as the heart and lungs) are all kept in place and supported by various parts of the skeleton.
- **Protection** – this is mainly provided by the flat bones, such as those in the cranium (skull) which protect the brain.
- **Movement** – the different types of joints allow different types of movement, as do the different types of bones.
- **Shape** – your overall shape and structure is provided by the skeleton and the two types of bones also affect the amount of movement possible. The short bones enable finer controlled movements (such as those in the fingers) and the longer bones enable gross (large) movements, such as those involving larger muscle groups, as in the legs when jumping, for example.
- **Mineral storage** – such as calcium, which helps with bone formation.
- **Blood cell production** – this takes place in the bone marrow where red blood cells are formed.

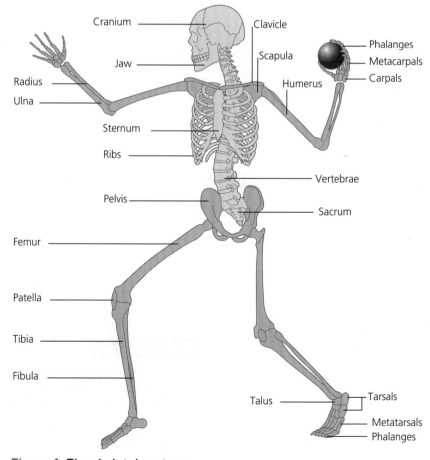

Figure 1 The skeletal system.

> ### Revision activity
>
> You can attempt this alone or with a partner. On your own body, or your partner's body, identify (or point to) as many specific named bones as you can. Print out the list of the ones you need to know to help you with this.

> ### Exam tip
>
> The examiner is not likely to ask questions relating to specific names of bones and their locations. However, they *are* likely to ask questions about how movement occurs and what types of movements these might be – including actual sporting examples!

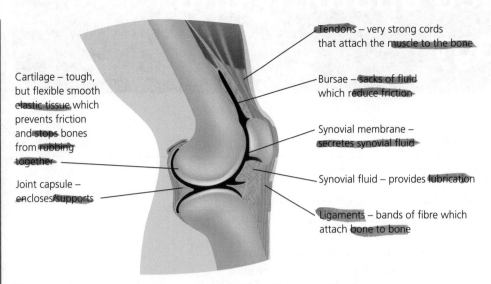

Tendons – very strong cords that attach the muscle to the bone

Cartilage – tough, but flexible smooth elastic tissue which prevents friction and stops bones from rubbing together

Bursae – sacks of fluid which reduce friction

Synovial membrane – secretes synovial fluid

Synovial fluid – provides lubrication

Joint capsule – encloses/supports

Ligaments – bands of fibre which attach bone to bone

Figure 2 The structure of a synovial joint, in this case the knee.

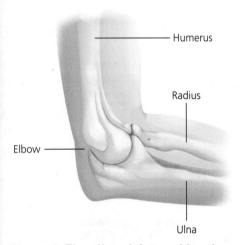

Humerus

Radius

Elbow

Ulna

Figure 3 The elbow joint enables the arm to bend and straighten.

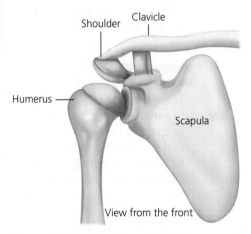

Shoulder
Clavicle

Humerus

Scapula

View from the front

Figure 4 The shoulder joint allows us to swing our arms and to move them outwards and inwards.

Typical mistake

Don't confuse abduction and adduction. Remember, if someone is taken away they are ABDucted and if you add something back in this is ADDed!

Specific bones and their location

The skeleton has **articulating bones**, which is where two or more bones meet at a **joint**, and it is important that you know both the location and identification of the following bones (which you can also see in Figure 1):

- head/neck: where the cranium and vertebrae are located
- shoulder: where the scapula and humerus are located
- chest: where the ribs and sternum are located
- elbow: where the humerus, radius and ulna are located
- hip: where the pelvis and femur are located
- knee: where the femur, tibia and patella are located
- ankle: where the tibia, fibula and talus are located.

Movement can only occur at the joints. There are different movements which can occur in each different freely movable joint:

- **Ball and socket** – these are the joints at the shoulder (scapula, clavicle and humerus) and the hips (femur and pelvis). The movements of **abduction** and **adduction** can take place here.
- **Hinge** – these are the joints at the knee (femur, patella and tibia), elbow (humerus, radius and ulna) and ankle (tibia, fibula and talus). The movements of **flexion** and **extension** occur here.

These joints are known as freely movable joints and they are the ones which allow the movements in sports actions to occur.

Hinge – KEA   Ball and socket – SH

Now test yourself   TESTED ☑

1. All of the following are functions of the skeleton except:
   a) size ✓
   b) support
   c) movement
   d) protection. (1 mark)
2. Bending your arm at the elbow is known as what?
   a) adduction
   b) flexion ✓
   c) extension
   d) abduction. (1 mark)
3. Which one of the following is an example of a hinge joint?
   a) shoulder
   b) hip
   c) knee ✓
   d) wrist. (1 mark)
4. Which three joints would be primarily involved in throwing a ball? (3 marks)

   Ball and socket
   hinge and
   shoulder, elbow, wrist.

In throwing a ball, the 3 joints that would be primarily used are shoulder elbow and wrist. This would be because as you go to throw the ball, your should rotates, your elbow moves from a flexed position to an extended position causing abduction on the wrist finally adding the last flick before releasing the ball.

Articulating bones Where two or more bones meet to allow movement at a joint

Joint A connection point between two bones where movement occurs

Abduction Movement away from the midline of the body – such as at the shoulder

Adduction Movement towards the midline of the body – such as at the shoulder

Flexion Decreasing the angle of the bones at a joint

Extension Increasing the angle of bones at a joint

Plantar flexion Pointing the toes at the ankle/increasing the ankle angle

Rotation Movement around an axis – such as at the shoulder

Exam tip

Remember that the skeletal system on its own cannot enable movement to occur. It must work in conjunction with the muscular system for this to happen. The skeletal system and muscular system working together is known as the musculoskeletal system.

1.2 Muscles of the body

The muscular system and skeletal system

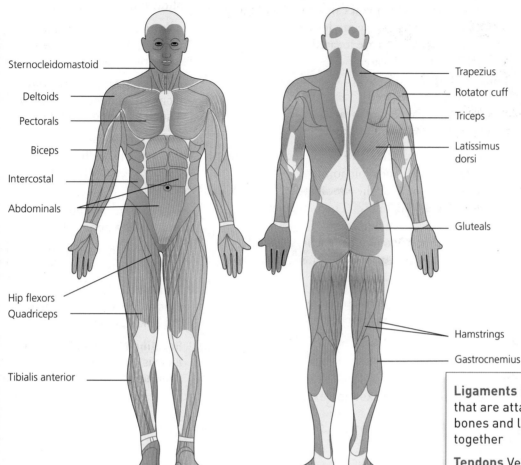

Figure 5 The main muscles of the body.

The muscular system and skeletal system combine to allow movement to occur. To do this they make use of connective tissues known as **ligaments** and **tendons**.

Muscles have to be arranged in pairs as they cannot push – they only pull:
- The prime mover (or **agonist**) is the muscle which initially contracts to start a movement.
- The **antagonist** is the muscle which relaxes to allow a movement to take place.

One example is the bending movement at the elbow. The antagonist would be the triceps, which relaxes and slightly lengthens (**eccentric contraction**), while the biceps would be the prime mover, as it contracts and appears to get smaller (**concentric contraction**) as it bulges. In the bicep curl, the eccentric phase of that exercise is in the action of lowering the dumbbell back down. You can feel these movements in your own arm if you grip loosely around the muscles.

Revision activity

You can attempt this alone or with a partner. On your own body, or on a partner's body, identify (or point to) as many specific named muscles as you can. Print out the list of the ones you need to know to help you with this.

Ligaments Bands of fibres that are attached to the bones and link the joints together

Tendons Very strong cords that join the muscle to the bone

Agonist Muscle or group of muscles responsible for movement

Antagonists Muscles that act to produce the opposite movement to the agonist. They work in antagonistic pairs

Eccentric contraction Lengthening of the muscle

Concentric contraction Shortening of the muscle

Typical mistake

Because we often carry out a pushing movement when we take part in physical activity, there is often confusion regarding whether muscles can push or not. They cannot – they only pull!

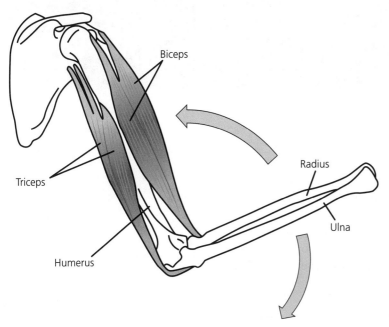

Labels in figure: Biceps, Triceps, Humerus, Radius, Ulna

Bursae Sacks of fluid which reduce friction

Cartilage Tough but flexible smooth elastic tissue which prevents friction and stops bones from rubbing together

Joint capsule Encloses/supports

Synovial fluid Provides lubrication

Synovial joint An area of the body where two or more bones meet (articulate) to allow a range of movements

Synovial membrane Secretes synovial fluid

Figure 6 Muscles bending at the elbow.

You only need to know about certain muscles and the main movements which occur at them:

- **Biceps and triceps** – any arm movements, such as throwing.
- **Hamstrings and quadriceps** – movements of the legs, such as running and kicking. Also **hip flexors**, **gluteals**, **gastrocnemius** and **tibialis anterior**.
- **Deltoids** – allow shoulder movement; used a lot in swimming.
- **Trapezius** – help to keep the shoulder in position; used in a soccer throw-in. Also **rotator cuffs**.
- **Latissimus dorsi** – allow shoulder movement backwards, forwards, up and down.
- **Pectorals** – at the front of the upper chest; often used in throwing actions such as the javelin.
- **Abdominals** – used to allow bending and turning of the trunk section; very important 'stabilising' muscles relating to 'core strength'.

Revision activity

Push against an object which you are able to move. Consider which muscles in your arms or legs (or both) were pulling, as the agonist(s), to allow that movement to occur.

Now test yourself

TESTED ☐

1 Which of the following best describes the role of tendons?
   a) they attach muscles to bones ✓
   b) they attach muscles to muscles
   c) they attach bones to bones
   d) they attach ligaments to bones. (1 mark)
2 The muscle which relaxes to allow a movement to take place is the:
   a) prime mover
   b) agonist
   c) flexor
   d) antagonist. (1 mark) ✓
3 Identify two major muscle groups of the upper body used when performing a standing throw of a ball. (2 marks)

BicePS, trapezius!

Exam tip

It is useful to know about certain muscles and the main movements that occur at them. However, exam questions will focus on how the muscular system is involved in movement and how the muscular and skeletal systems combine together to allow movement.

1b The structure and function of the cardio-respiratory system

1.3 The cardio-respiratory system

REVISED

The pathway of air

Gaseous exchange occurs in the alveoli and it is important to be aware of the key features of this process:

- The large surface area of the alveoli greatly assists this process.
- The alveoli consist of moist thin walls which are only one cell thick.
- There is only a very short distance for the gases to travel for diffusion – this is known as the short diffusion pathway.
- There are a great number of capillaries.
- The large blood supply enables the process to be more efficient.
- The actual movement of the gas is from high concentrations to low concentrations.

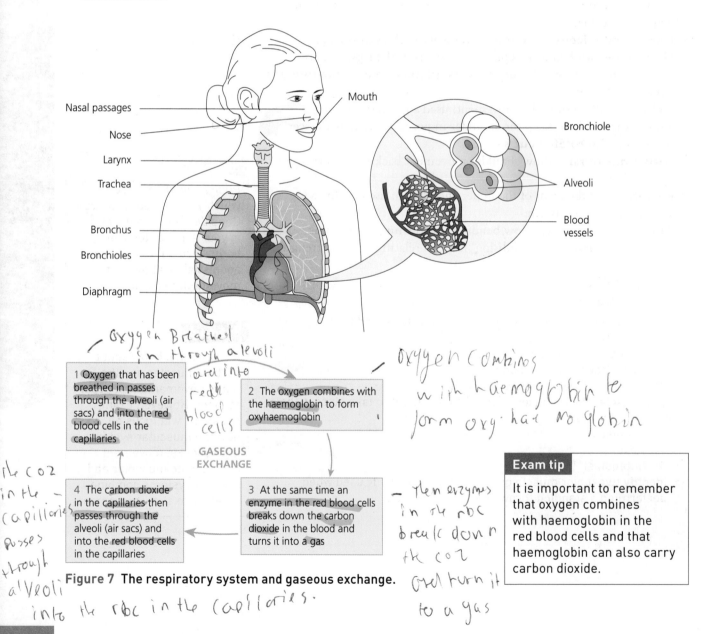

Oxygen Breathed in through alveoli and into red blood cells

1 Oxygen that has been breathed in passes through the alveoli (air sacs) and into the red blood cells in the capillaries

oxygen combines with haemoglobin to form oxy·hae mo globin

2 The oxygen combines with the haemoglobin to form oxyhaemoglobin

GASEOUS EXCHANGE

the co2 in the capillaries passes through alveoli into the rbc in the capillaries.

4 The carbon dioxide in the capillaries then passes through the alveoli (air sacs) and into the red blood cells in the capillaries

3 At the same time an enzyme in the red blood cells breaks down the carbon dioxide in the blood and turns it into a gas

then enzymes in the rbc break down the co2 and turn it to a gas

Figure 7 The respiratory system and gaseous exchange.

Exam tip

It is important to remember that oxygen combines with haemoglobin in the red blood cells and that haemoglobin can also carry carbon dioxide.

Mechanics of breathing

In order for breathing to happen there is an interaction of the intercostal muscles, the rib cage and the diaphragm, which results in air being breathed into and out of the lungs.

When you are at rest and inhaling (**inspiring**), the diaphragm flattens and moves downwards and the intercostal muscles contract, which raises the ribs up, making the chest cavity larger. This has the effect of reducing the air pressure inside the chest cavity, which in turn causes air to be sucked into the lungs.

The reverse process happens when you are exhaling (**expiring**), and you can see from the figure below that the diaphragm becomes dome shaped, which effectively makes the chest cavity smaller.

When you are exercising, the lungs can expand more when you are inspiring than they do when you are at rest. This is due to the paired muscle action of the pectorals and sternocleidomastoid at the side of the neck. When you then expire, the rib cage is pulled down much more quickly to force the air out faster due to the movement of the abdominal muscles.

> **Inspiring** Breathing in
>
> **Expiring** Breathing out

Exam tip

Remember that inhalation (breathing in) and exhalation (breathing out) occur due to changes in air pressure which enable these processes to take place.

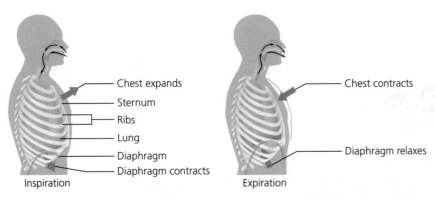

Inspiration — Chest expands, Sternum, Ribs, Lung, Diaphragm, Diaphragm contracts

Expiration — Chest contracts, Diaphragm relaxes

Figure 8 Inspiration and expiration – breathing in and out.

Air pressure and a spirometer trace

A spirometer trace is a measure of lung volumes which includes:

- **tidal volume:** the volume of air inspired or expired/exchanged in each breath
- **inspiratory reserve volume:** the amount of air that could be breathed in after tidal volume
- **expiratory reserve volume:** the amount of air that could be breathed out after tidal volume
- **residual volume:** the amount of air left in the lungs after maximal expiration.

Exam tip

You may be shown a spirometer trace and asked to interpret and explain it. The amount of air you inspire and expire changes between rest and the onset of exercise. Tidal volume increases with exercise, expiratory reserve volume decreases during exercise (as does inspiratory reserve volume) and residual volume stays the same with no change during exercise.

Revision activity

Carry out an internet search for an actual example of a spirometer trace and look at the four different identified volumes which are explained above.

The structure of the heart

The heart is basically a muscular pump which acts in the way shown in Figure 9 to complete the cardiac cycle and for the pathway of the blood to occur.

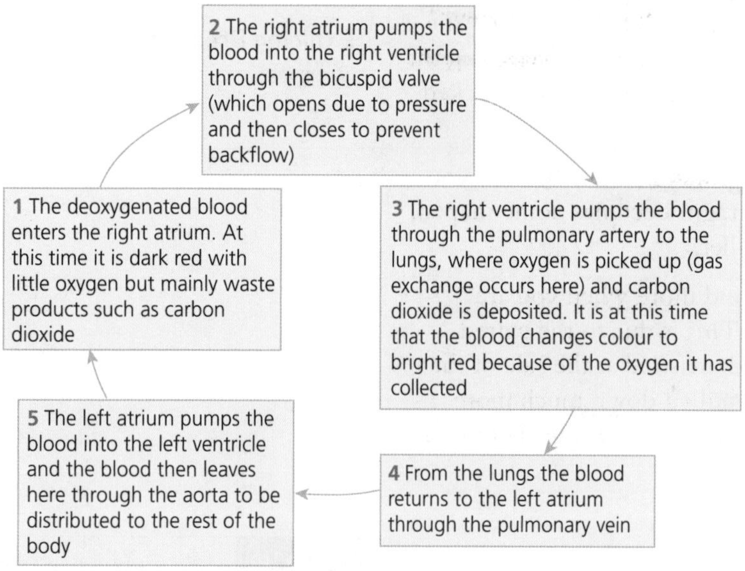

2 The right atrium pumps the blood into the right ventricle through the bicuspid valve (which opens due to pressure and then closes to prevent backflow)
1 The deoxygenated blood enters the right atrium. At this time it is dark red with little oxygen but mainly waste products such as carbon dioxide
3 The right ventricle pumps the blood through the pulmonary artery to the lungs, where oxygen is picked up (gas exchange occurs here) and carbon dioxide is deposited. It is at this time that the blood changes colour to bright red because of the oxygen it has collected
5 The left atrium pumps the blood into the left ventricle and the blood then leaves here through the aorta to be distributed to the rest of the body
4 From the lungs the blood returns to the left atrium through the pulmonary vein

Figure 9 The cardiac cycle.

Vena cava
Pulmonary artery
Aorta
Left atrium
Pulmonary vein
Right atrium
Bicuspid valve
Semi-lunar valve
Semi-lunar valve
Left ventricle
Tricuspid valve
Right ventricle
Septum
Vena cava

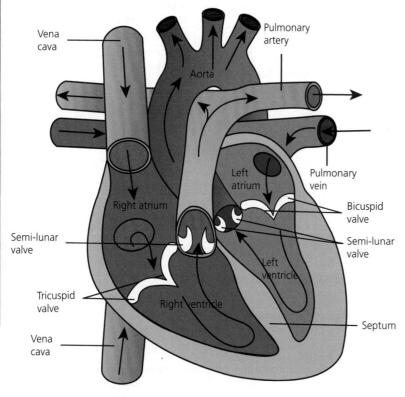

Figure 10 The heart.

Cardiac cycle The process of the heart going through the stages of systole and diastole in the atria and ventricles

Diastolic blood pressure When the heart is relaxing

Embolism The blockage of a blood vessel

Haemoglobin The substance in red blood cells which transports oxygen (as oxyhaemoglobin) and carbon dioxide

Hypertension High blood pressure in the arteries

Systolic blood pressure When the heart is contracting

Vasoconstriction Narrowing of the internal diameter of a blood vessel to decrease blood flow, such as the arteries constricting during exercise so that less blood is delivered to inactive areas

Vasodilation Widening of the internal diameter of a blood vessel to increase blood flow, such as the arteries dilating during exercise so that more blood is delivered to active areas, effectively increasing their oxygen supply

Exam tip

The examiner will not ask specific questions about the heart and its chambers. However, knowing how the blood is transported throughout the body via the blood vessels will help you to answer questions relating to effective training methods, the effect of exercise on the body and the redistribution of blood during exercise (vasoconstriction and vasodilation).

Blood vessels

There are three types of blood vessels in our bodies:

- **Arteries** – these have thick walls and carry oxygenated blood at high pressure away from the heart. They have no valves and have more elastic walls than veins. They sub-divide into smaller vessels known as arterioles.
- **Veins** – these carry deoxygenated blood back to the heart and have thinner, less elastic walls than arteries. Veins have valves to make sure that the blood is not able to flow backwards.
- **Capillaries** – these are microscopic vessels that allow carbon dioxide, oxygen and waste products to pass through their very thin walls.

Cardiac output, stroke volume and heart rate

It is important that you know and understand the relationship between cardiac output, stroke volume and heart rate. The formula for this is as follows:

Cardiac output (Q) = stroke volume × heart rate

- Cardiac output (Q) is the amount of blood which is ejected from the heart in one minute – also shown as stroke volume × heart rate.
- Stroke volume is the amount of blood pumped out of the heart by each ventricle during one contraction.
- Heart rate is the number of times the heart beats, and is usually measured in beats per minute.

Exam tip

You may be asked to interpret a heart rate graph. If so, you need to be aware that an anticipatory rise is where the heart rate starts to rise slightly before any exercise starts and changes in intensity occur according to the levels of demand which various levels of exercise or exercises have.

Typical mistake

Students often think that the process of breathing only occurs in the lungs. It is far more complex than that and what happens in the lungs is only part of the process.

Now test yourself

TESTED

1 Which of the following is not a blood vessel?
   a) plasma
   b) capillary
   c) vein
   d) artery. (1 mark)
2 Explain the differences between an artery and a vein. (4 marks)
3 Which of the following is the volume of air inspired/exchanged per breath?
   a) residual volume
   b) tidal volume
   c) expiratory reserve volume
   d) inspiratory reserve volume. (1 mark)
4 Explain the interaction of the intercostal muscles, ribs and diaphragm when at rest and inhaling. (4 marks)

[Handwritten annotations:]

A — Away

thick walls, carry oxygenated blood at high pressures away from heart, plastic walls.

→ carry de oxygenated blood back to heart., thinner less elastic walls

2) An artery is a type of blood vessel that carries oxy blood away from the heart. at a high pressure it also has higher elastic walls or thicker

A vein is a type of blood vessel that carries de oxygenated blood to the heart, it has thinner or less elastic walls.

when you are at rest and inhaling your dia phram moves downwards and flattens, your intercostal muscles contract, therfore your ribs more out wards and you chest cavity expards.
Bay
→ more upwards
Or causes air to be sucked in

1c Anaerobic and aerobic exercise

1.4 Anaerobic and aerobic exercise

REVISED

Anaerobic exercise

[handwritten: — Glucose → energy + lactic acid]

[handwritten left margin: weight lifting, sprinter]

Anaerobic respiration is respiration in the absence of oxygen and is summarised as:

Glucose → energy + lactic acid

This type of respiration is used when the body works without sufficient oxygen being supplied to the muscles. As oxygen is not being used to generate the energy, anaerobic respiration can only be used for short periods of exercise.

Aerobic exercise

[handwritten: — Glucose + oxygen → energy + carbon dioxide + water]

[handwritten left margin: Marathon runner, swimmer, cyclist – long race, footballer, golfer – golf putt]

Aerobic respiration is respiration in the presence of oxygen and is summarised as:

Glucose + oxygen → energy + carbon dioxide + water

This type of respiration is used when the body is exercising for a long period of time and the energy for this exercise is produced using oxygen. Aerobic exercise makes full use of the respiratory system to make sure that sufficient oxygen is being taken in throughout the exercise period.

> **Exam tip**
>
> Make sure you know the difference between aerobic and anaerobic exercise and can give an example of each. Learn the formulas for both types of respiration.

> **Revision activity**
>
> Make yourself a list of at least five sports or activities that you would consider to be anaerobic exercise and five which you would consider to be aerobic exercise.

A 100 metre sprinter is a good example of anaerobic exercise – in the absence of oxygen.

A marathon runner is a good example of aerobic exercise – in the presence of oxygen.

EPOC (oxygen debt)

Excess post-exercise oxygen consumption (EPOC) occurs during anaerobic exercise. This is because as the body runs out of sufficient supplies of oxygen, the glycogen stores are used as an alternative energy supply. Lactic acid (a mild poison) builds up in the working muscles. Oxygen debt is the additional oxygen consumption during recovery above what is usually required when at rest. The performer is therefore required to maintain an increased breathing rate after exercise to repay this debt.

The recovery process from vigorous exercise

Straight after exercise the body has to be allowed to recover. It is important to know the following methods and the reasons they are used to help this recovery process:
- **Cool-down** – this allows the lactic acid to disperse safely and helps to maintain the elevated breathing rate and heart rate (and therefore the blood flow). Including some gentle stretching as part of this process is also beneficial.
- **Manipulation of diet** – this includes ensuring that you rehydrate, and it is also advisable to take on carbohydrates as an additional energy source.
- **Ice baths/massage** – the main reason for performers using this method is to prevent delayed onset muscle soreness (DOMS). Massage, in particular, helps to increase blood flow to the sore area.

Exam tip

You need to know about these methods and also be able to justify why they would be relevant in different sporting activities. Just about every activity requires a cool-down and this is often a repeat of some of the activities used in the warm-up. Endurance athletes often make use of diet manipulation as well as ice baths and massage.

Typical mistake

The most common mistake is getting the terms aerobic and anaerobic muddled up. An easy way to remember is that someone taking part in an aerobics class, or session, will be working for a long period of time, not a short time.

Now test yourself
TESTED

1 Anaerobic respiration will be used in a:
   a) marathon run
   b) 100 metre sprint
   c) cross-country run
   d) 100 metre swimming race. (1 mark)
2 What is lactic acid and how can you effectively remove it from the body? (4 marks)
3 Describe three different methods used to recover from vigorous exercise. (6 marks)

[Handwritten answers:]

2) lactic acid is a mild poison that is present in working muscles after exercise. A way to effectively remove it is to have a cool down after an event to let it disperse safely, another is to have a massage to shift the lactic acid and another is to gently stretch.

3) one method used to recover is a cool down, this is where you either do some gentle stretching to prevent chances of injury, you could also slowly jog to let the lactic acid disperse safley.

- Another method is a manipulation of diet, this is where you ensure that after you vigorously exercise you rehydrate, and make sure before events that you eat carbohydrates.

- A final method is to have an ice bath or massage, this is effectively to prevent delayed onset muscle soreness (DOMS) and a massage in particular helps the shift of lactic acid and increase rate of blood flow to the sore areas.

6/6

1.5 The effects of exercise

Immediate effects

These are the effects which are felt immediately during exercise:

- a feeling of being hot (certainly hotter than at rest)
- increased levels of sweating and perspiring
- an increase in both the depth and frequency of breathing (the average resting rate is 14–16 breaths a minute, so it will increase from this)
- an increased heart rate from the normal resting rate, which on average is 72 beats a minute.

Short-term effects

The short-term period is between 24 and 36 hours after exercise has taken place, and the potential effects are:

- increased tiredness or **fatigue**
- a feeling of lightheadedness
- nausea
- aching and DOMS
- **cramp**.

Cramp can also occur during an activity so it is not just a short-term effect.

Long-term effects

One of the main reasons for anyone to exercise regularly is to be able to enjoy the benefits which can be gained after months and years of exercising. These can include:

- Body shape may change: this could be as basic as losing weight but for others it could be toning or building muscle.
- Improvements in specific components of fitness (see Section 3.2 on page 22).
- Building muscle strength.
- Improved **muscular endurance**; this could then reduce the short-term effects of fatigue previously experienced.

> **Revision activity**
>
> The next time you, or a fellow student, are exercising make a conscious note (or observe and write down) what the immediate effects of exercise are. If possible, attempt to come up with some way of measuring them – breathing rate for example.

> **Fatigue** Either physical or mental, it is a feeling of extreme or severe tiredness, due to a build-up of lactic acid or working for long periods of time
>
> **Cramp** A sudden, involuntary contraction of a muscle or muscle group
>
> **Muscular endurance** The ability of a muscle or muscle group to undergo repeated contractions, avoiding fatigue

> **Exam tip**
>
> When you are considering, or revising, the long-term effects of exercise you must be able to link them to the identified components of fitness (see Section 3.2, page 22) as exam questions are likely to be set relating to specific components and the effects that exercise has on them.

> **Typical mistake**
>
> The effects felt as a result of exercise may be slightly unpleasant at times but this is not a reason for not exercising. The overall effects of exercise are all positive ones.

- Improved speed.
- Improved **suppleness**.
- Building **cardio-vascular endurance**.
- Improving **stamina**.
- Increasing the size of the heart and therefore **hypertrophy**.
- A lower resting heart rate, also known as **bradycardia**.

Now test yourself

TESTED ☐

1 Which of the following is not a long-term effect of exercise?
   a) change in body shape
   b) improved stamina
   c) increased heart rate
   d) improved suppleness. (1 mark)
2 What is meant by hypertrophy of the heart and why would this be a benefit to a specific performer? (5 marks)
3 Describe three different short-term effects of exercise. (6 marks)

Suppleness Another term for flexibility, the range of movement possible at a joint

Cardio-vascular endurance The ability of the heart and lungs to supply oxygen to the working muscles, also known as aerobic power

Stamina The ability to exert yourself and keep active for long periods of time

Hypertrophy The enlargement of an organ or tissue from the increase in the size of its cells

Bradycardia The heart beating very slowly at rest, at or below 60 beats a minute

Summary

This chapter concentrates on the human body and movement in physical activity and sport. It is important that after reading this chapter you are able to develop your knowledge and understanding of the key body systems and that you are able to apply this basic knowledge of anatomy and physiology.

The main areas for you to review, revise and be aware of are as follows:
- The major bones of the body and where they are located.
- The structure of the skeleton, concentrating on its principal function of providing a framework for movement. Remember that this movement only occurs when the skeletal system works with the muscular system!
- The specific functions of the skeleton and being able to link these functions in an applied way to performances in physical activities.
- The major muscles of the body, their location and the important role of tendons which attach the muscle to bone.
- The structure of an actual synovial joint; the knee is the most common and clearest example of these. This knowledge should be linked to the ways in which structures within these joints help to prevent injury.
- The most common types of freely movable joints, specifically at the elbow, knee, ankle, hip and shoulder.
- How the joints differ for particular types of movement to occur. Remember that movement can only occur at a joint and that muscles are always in pairs as they cannot push, they only pull to allow this movement to take place!

- The pathway of air, in the respiratory system in particular.
- What gaseous exchange is and where it occurs – remember that the two gases are oxygen (not air!) and carbon dioxide.
- The major blood vessels in the circulatory system and how the structure of these blood vessels is linked to their functions.
- The structure of the heart, the cardiac cycle and the pathway of the blood. Remember that the primary function of the heart is to act as a pump, pumping the blood around the body.
- Being able to interpret a heart rate graph in terms of cardiac output, stroke volume and heart rate.
- The mechanics of breathing and especially the interaction of the intercostal muscles, ribs and diaphragm in breathing.
- Being able to interpret a spirometer trace which shows the change from rest to exercise.
- Understanding what is meant by anaerobic and aerobic exercise and being able to link these terms to practical examples of sporting situations. Remember, some sports or activities have phases where either anaerobic or aerobic exercise can be used!
- Understanding what delayed onset muscle soreness (DOMS) is and what can cause it, as well as being able to link this with the recovery process from vigorous exercise.
- The effects of exercise experienced immediately, in the short term and in the long term. Be sure to consider this topic in relation to the components of fitness covered in Chapter 3.

2 Movement analysis

2.1 Lever systems and mechanical advantage

REVISED

Lever systems

You need to be able to identify **lever** systems and to be able to give examples of their use in activity. There are three different types of levers which you need to be able to identify, as well as being able to give examples of their use in physical activity and sport. The details regarding these three different types are given below.

First class levers

A first class lever has the fulcrum lying between the effort and the resistance. An example of this is the way the triceps muscle of the arm acts during extension, such as the movement performed when throwing a ball.

The elbow joint is a very good example of a first class lever, especially when flexing and extending (see Figure 2). Throwing a javelin is an example of a first class lever in action.

> **Lever** A rigid bar (bone) that turns about an axis to create movement. The effort (also known as force) to move the lever comes from the muscle(s). Each lever contains a fulcrum, which is the fixed point the lever is placed on and it requires effort (from the muscles) to move it. The lever also contains the load/resistance from gravity

> **Exam tip**
>
> You could be required to make a basic drawing of the three classes of levers. For each one you must be able to clearly label the fulcrum, load (resistance) and effort.

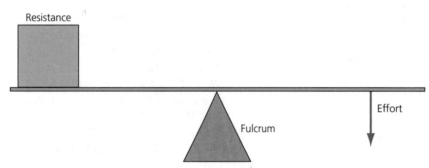

Figure 1 First class lever.

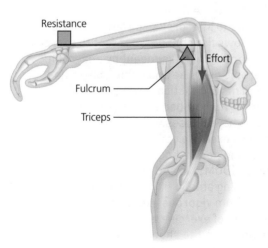

Figure 2 The first class lever system at the elbow joint.

Second class levers

A second class lever is one where the fulcrum lies at one end with the effort at the other end. The resistance then lies in the middle of the effort and the fulcrum. An example of this is at the ankle, where the gastrocnemius causes plantar flexion, such as the movement performed when taking a set shot at basketball.

The ankle joint is a very good example of a second class lever when plantar flexion takes place (see Figure 4). Pushing off the ground to complete a set shot at basketball would be an example of a second class lever in action.

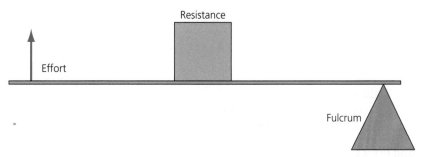

Figure 3 Second class lever.

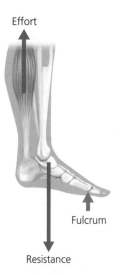

Figure 4 The second class lever system at the ankle joint.

Third class levers

A third class lever is one where the fulcrum is located at one end and the resistance is at the other end, with the effort located between the fulcrum and the resistance, such as the movement when performing a biceps curl.

The elbow moving a resistance in the hand is a good example of a third class lever. Paddling a kayak is an example of a third class lever in action.

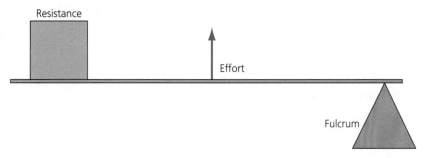

Figure 5 Third class lever.

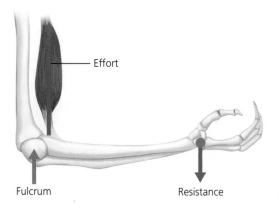

Figure 6 The third class lever system at the elbow joint.

Typical mistake

Considering that force and effort are two separate things; when related to lever systems they are the same thing.

Revision activity

Practise drawing each of the three classes of lever in the simple diagram form above, making sure that you are able to accurately identify and label the fulcrum, load and effort in each one.

Exam tip

You will not be required to draw anatomical body parts but you do need to be able to link each correct lever system to a specific sporting movement or action.

Mechanical advantage

Mechanical advantage is very closely linked to the three classes of levers, and the interpretation of the mechanical advantage of that lever, and this can be seen in the diagram below.

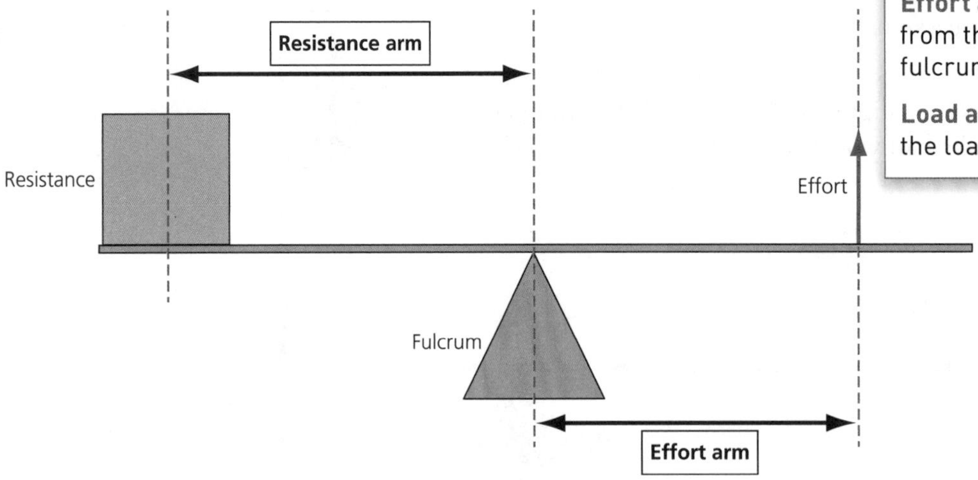

Figure 7 The idea of resistance arm and effort arm.

When a lever's effort arm is longer than its load arm it is said to have a **high mechanical advantage**. Levers with high mechanical advantage can move large loads with relatively low effort. Second class levers always have high mechanical advantage.

When a lever's arm is longer than its effort arm, it has low mechanical advantage. Third class levers always have **low mechanical advantage**.

First class levers can have high mechanical advantage if the fulcrum is closer to the load, but if the fulcrum is closer to the effort then they will have low mechanical advantage.

> **Mechanical advantage**
> The efficiency of a working lever, calculated by effort ÷ weight (resistance) arm
>
> **Effort arm** The distance from the effort to the fulcrum
>
> **Load arm** The distance from the load to the fulcrum

> **Revision activity**
>
> Practice labelling the **effort arm** and **load arm** on the three classes of levers. It is important that you are able to complete this accurately. Also, note the level of mechanical advantage for each example you label.

Now test yourself

TESTED

1 Which of the following would *not* be considered to be part of a lever system?
   a) advantage
   b) effort
   c) load
   d) fulcrum. (1 mark)
2 Which of the following is *not* true of a lever class?
   a) second class levers always have high mechanical advantage
   b) first class levers never have low mechanical advantage
   c) first class levers can have high mechanical advantage
   d) third class levers always have low mechanical advantage. (1 mark)
3 Explain what a lever system is. (3 marks)
4 How is it possible to work out mechanical advantage? (3 marks)

2.2 Basic movements and planes and axes of movement

REVISED

This section links very closely with Sections 1.1 and 1.2 (the muscular and skeletal systems on pages 1 and 4) as it adds more information and detail to movement at a joint and the seven specific identified movements you need to know.

Movement analysis

For analysis of basic movements, it must be remembered that many movements occur in opposite directions, which is why many of the movements above are 'paired off' when they occur at the major joints, as listed below:

- **flexion** or **extension**: frequently occurs at the shoulder, elbow, hip and knee
- **abduction** or **adduction**: occurs at the shoulder
- **rotation** at the shoulder: because this is an all-round circular movement there is no 'pairing' here
- **plantar flexion** or **dorsiflexion**: at the ankle.

You need to be able to link specific sporting actions to the type of movement which occurs, taking into account the information above. The following examples are the basic ones you need to know:

- The **elbow action** which occurs performing push-ups (press-ups) and also when taking a football throw-in (Figure 8).
- The **hip, knee and ankle action** which occurs in running, kicking, the standing vertical jump (see Section 3.2, page 22) (the vertical test jump, Figure 9) and basic squats.
- The **shoulder action** during cricket bowling, which involves overarm rotation (Figure 10).

Figure 8 The movements during a push-up.

> **Revision activity**
>
> Make sure that you have either read (or re-read) Sections 1.1 and 1.2 before you go on to read this chapter. Be prepared to go back to both of those sections as you work through this chapter.

> **Flexion** Decreasing the angle of the bones at a joint
>
> **Extension** Increasing the angle of bones at a joint
>
> **Abduction** Movement away from the midline of the body
>
> **Adduction** Movement towards the midline of the body
>
> **Rotation** Movement around an axis
>
> **Plantar flexion** Pointing the toes down at the ankle/increasing the ankle angle
>
> **Dorsiflexion** Pulling the toes up at the ankle/decreasing the ankle angle

> **Exam tip**
>
> Questions relating to this section are very much focused on you being able to apply your knowledge of anatomy and physiology! This is why you will need to constantly refer back to Chapter 1 and the anatomy and physiology content there.

A **B**

Figure 9 Standing vertical jump.

Figure 10 Shoulder action during cricket bowling.

A **B**

Figure 11 You can clearly see the flexion and extension which occurs at the shoulder in order for the throw-in to be successful.

> **Axis** Imaginary line through the body around which it rotates; there are three types of axis
>
> **Longitudinal axis** Head to toe
>
> **Transverse axis** Through the hips
>
> **Sagittal axis** Through the belly button
>
> **Plane** Imaginary line depicting the direction of movement; there are three types of plane
>
> **Sagittal plane** Forwards and backwards
>
> **Frontal plane** Left or right
>
> **Transverse plane** Rotation around the longitudinal axis

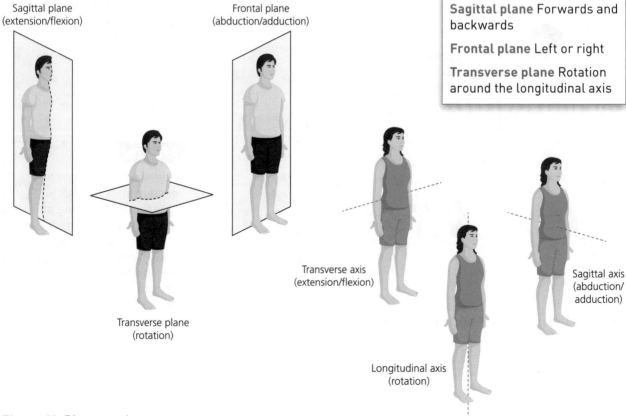

Sagittal plane (extension/flexion)

Frontal plane (abduction/adduction)

Transverse plane (rotation)

Transverse axis (extension/flexion)

Sagittal axis (abduction/ adduction)

Longitudinal axis (rotation)

Figure 12 Planes and axes.

Planes and axes of movement

You need to be able identify the relevant planes and axes of movement which are used while performing sporting actions.

The following list of actions are the ones you should be aware of:

- the front somersault, forward roll, running action
- the 360° twist, such as ice-skater spin or a discus thrower rotating in a circle
- a cartwheel.

Typical mistake

That an axis and axes are completely different terms. Axes is the plural of axis so they are effectively exactly the same term.

Revision activity

Using Figure 12, showing the planes and axes of movement, draw the list of actions identified and match the different planes and axes to the three different examples. Simple matchstick-person drawing will be enough.

Now test yourself   TESTED ☑

1 Which of the following is the correct description of rotation?
   a) movement towards the midline of the body *adduction* ✓
   b) movement away from the midline of the body *abduction*
   c) increasing the angle of bones at a joint *extension* ✓
   d) movement around an axis. (1 mark) *rotation.*
2 Which of the following is *not* a plane?
   a) longitudinal —— ✓
   b) frontal
   c) sagittal
   d) transverse. (1 mark)
3 Describe the elbow action in a football throw-in. (3 marks)
4 Identify the relevant planes and axes used when performing a cartwheel. (3 marks) ☒ *In my notebook*

Summary

This chapter concentrates on developing your knowledge and understanding of the basic principles of movement and their effect on performance in physical activity and sport.

The main areas for you to review, revise and be aware of are as follows:

- Understanding what is meant by first, second and third class levers, and being able to link the correct lever to a sporting movement or action.
- Understanding what is meant by the term mechanical advantage and the relationship this has with the three different types of levers.
- Understanding the different types of basic movements and relating these to specific sporting examples.
- Understanding the three relevant planes of movement: frontal, transverse and sagittal. Being able to relate these to sporting examples.
- Understanding the three relevant axes of movement: longitudinal, transverse and sagittal. Being able to relate these to sporting examples.

3 Physical training

3.1 Health and fitness

REVISED

There is a very close relationship between **health** and fitness.

An individual's fitness level may decrease if they are experiencing **ill health** because a level of poor health can affect the ability to train and this, in turn, would lower the levels of **fitness**.

It is possible for an individual to increase their fitness levels despite being in poor health if they are still able to train which, in turn, can result in fitness levels increasing.

The components of fitness

Fitness is not just one physical attribute as it consists of a number of factors, broken down into components, which are either skill-related or health-related factors:

- **Agility** – the ability to move and change direction quickly (at speed) while maintaining control. This can also be considered to be a combination of flexibility and speed.
- **Balance** – the maintenance of the centre of mass over the base of support. This includes static balances (maintained while still and not moving) and dynamic (when moving).
- **Cardio-vascular endurance** (also known as **aerobic power**; see Section 1.5, page 12) – the ability of the heart and lungs to supply oxygen to the working muscles.

> **Health** A state of complete physical, mental and social well-being, and not merely the absence of disease or infirmity
>
> **Ill health** A state of poor physical, mental and/or social well-being
>
> **Fitness** The ability to meet or cope with the demands of the environment

This gymnast is effectively combining flexibility, balance and static strength in this controlled movement.

- **Co-ordination** – the ability to use different (two or more) parts of the body together, smoothly and efficiently.
- **Flexibility** – the range of movements possible at a joint.
- **Muscular endurance** – this is similar to dynamic strength and is the ability of a muscle or muscle group to undergo repeated contractions, avoiding fatigue.
- **Power** (also known as **explosive strength** or **anaerobic power**) – the product of strength and speed: strength × speed.
- **Reaction time** – the time taken to initiate a response to a stimulus, that is, the time from the initiation of the stimulus (for example the starting gun firing in a race) to starting to initiate a response (for example starting to move out of the blocks in response to the sound of the starting gun).
- **Speed** – the maximum rate at which an individual is able to perform a movement or cover a distance in a period of time, putting the body parts into action as quickly as possible. This is calculated as distance ÷ time.
- **Strength** – the ability to overcome a resistance, broken down into the following sub-categories:
  - **maximal strength** – the maximum force that a muscle can exert in a single voluntary contraction
  - **explosive** – the muscular strength used in one short, sharp movement (closely linked with power)
  - **static** – the ability to hold a body part (limb) in a static position; the muscle length stays the same and it is the maximum force which can be applied to an immovable object
  - **dynamic** – also known as muscular endurance (see definition above).

Typical mistake

Referring to reaction time as 'the time it takes to react'. That is just a rearrangement of the component wording. It is a better answer to refer to responding to a stimulus.

Exam tip

It is essential that you are able to remember each of the ten definitions of fitness (and be aware of the alternative terms, such as cardio-vascular endurance also being known as aerobic power) and that you are able to link each of these to a particular sport or physical activity.

Revision activity

Create a table where you list all ten components of fitness with at least one linked sport or physical activity. This is an example to get you started: **flexibility**, linked to the sport of **gymnastics** and/ or the activity of **hurdling**.

Now test yourself

TESTED ☐

1 All of the following are types of strength apart from:
   a) static
   b) enduring
   c) dynamic
   d) explosive. (1 mark)
2 Flexibility is best described as:
   a) having bendy bones
   b) moving at a joint
   c) the range of movement an individual has
   d) the range of movements possible at a joint. (1 mark)
3 All of the following would be an advantage to a sprinter apart from:
   a) endurance
   b) reaction time
   c) explosive strength
   d) speed. (1 mark)
4 What is meant by good reaction time and how would this be of particular advantage to a 100 m sprinter? (4 marks)

[Handwritten notes:]

✱ gaining the max adv.

3/4
— explain it
getting off blocks first,
getting into stride ✱

— reaction time is the time taken to initiate to a stimulus, this is an advantage to a sprinter as you need to react quickly to the starting gun ✓ to gain an advantage ✓. However a disadvantage of this could be that you may go too quickly eg before the gun and be disqualified ✱ so a more important one is speed and strength and can give you a better start. ✱

3.2 Measuring the components of fitness

Reasons for carrying out fitness tests

Testing levels of fitness, and specific components of fitness, is vital for all performers from beginner to elite level. The reasons for this include:

- to be able identify strengths and/or weaknesses, either in a performance or to gauge the success of a training programme
- to monitor improvement
- to show a starting level of fitness
- to inform training requirements
- to compare against norms of the group or national averages
- to motivate and set goals
- to provide variety to a training programme.

There can be limitations to fitness testing. These will vary according to the particular test but they include the following:

- tests are often not sport-specific or are too general
- they may not replicate movements of the actual activity
- they do not replicate competitive conditions required in sports
- many do not use direct measuring or are sub-maximal and are therefore inaccurate as some of the tests require levels of motivation and others have questionable reliability
- these tests must be carried out with the correct procedures to increase their validity.

Each of the components of fitness has an associated test which is used to measure that particular component. These are as follows:

- **agility** – the Illinois agility test (Figure 1)
- **balance** – the stork balance test (Figure 2)
- **cardio-vascular endurance** (aerobic power) – the multi-stage fitness test (Figure 3)
- **co-ordination** – the wall toss test (Figure 4)
- **flexibility** – the sit and reach test (Figure 5)
- **muscular endurance** – the sit-up bleep test (Figure 6)
- **power/explosive strength** (anaerobic power) – the vertical jump test (Figure 7)
- **reaction time** – the ruler drop test (Figure 8)
- **maximal strength** – the one rep max test (Figure 9)
- **speed** – the 30 m sprint test (Figure 10)
- **strength** – the handgrip dynamometer test (Figure 11).

Exam tip

As part of the performance analysis assessment for the practical component there is a requirement to identify strengths and weaknesses of 'a fitness component'. The only way this is possible is through being able to both measure and test that component.

Typical mistake

That 'fitness' can be tested. Only the specific components can be tested – there is no single test for fitness.

Exam tip

The best way for you to learn, understand and be able to describe these tests is to actually attempt to take each one of them. It would also be best to do this towards the start of your course (in Year 9/10) and then again towards the end of the course (Year 11) so that you can produce some of your own data which you can then look at different ways of presenting. You can even compare this data to other members of your PE group and track your own progress and development as well.

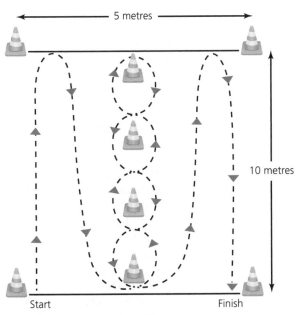

Figure 1 The Illinois agility test.

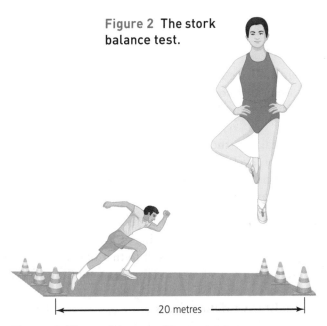

Figure 2 The stork balance test.

Figure 3 The multi-stage fitness test.

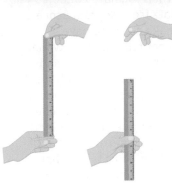

Figure 4 The wall toss test.

Figure 5 The sit and reach test.

Figure 6 The sit-up bleep test.

Figure 7 The vertical jump test.

Figure 8 The ruler drop test.

Figure 9 The one rep max test.

Figure 10 The 30 m sprint test.

Figure 11 The handgrip dynamometer test.

Demonstrating how data is collected for fitness testing

When you have carried out the eleven fitness tests outlined above it, is important that you clearly understand how the test scores you got were actually measured and/or recorded. The main variations and methods will be:

- time taken – such as seconds, or minutes and seconds
- level or levels attained
- distances or heights attained – such as centimetres and metres
- numbers achieved.

You should be able not only to record your test score but also to demonstrate your understanding of the method used to attain your score, and to compare your test result to that of national averages. When you are doing this you also need to understand the two types of data that you may have recorded, these are:

- **Qualitative data** – this is more of a **subjective** than an **objective** appraisal. This would therefore involve opinions relating to the quality of a performance rather than the quantity (such as the score you achieved, the placing you achieved or the number you attained). Note that none of the eleven fitness tests above would result in you attaining qualitative data but if you took part in a gymnastics competition where judges were scoring your routine then this would be qualitative data.
- **Quantitative data** – this is a measurement which can be quantified as a number, such as a time in seconds or goals scored or achieved. There are no opinions expressed (as this would be qualitative) as it is a fact.

Revision activity

Create your own detailed table which sets out the procedure for carrying out each of the eleven fitness tests. Try to include all of the following in this:

- the facilities and equipment needed to set the test up
- the tasks and rules of the test and the procedures which have to be followed
- any measurements or tables which are used to actually score/rate the performance
- the way in which conclusions are drawn from the results or scores obtained.

Subjective Existing in the mind

Objective Not influenced by personal feelings but based on facts

Now test yourself

TESTED ☐

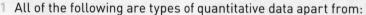

1 All of the following are types of quantitative data apart from:
  a) time taken
  b) score achieved
  c) judged performance
  d) placing attained. (1 mark)
2 The ruler drop test is a test for:
  a) speed
  b) reaction time
  c) co-ordination
  d) agility. (1 mark)
3 Describe, in full, what the sit and reach test consists of and explain which component of fitness it is designed to test. (6 marks)

Revision activity

When you have collected data from any test scores, make sure you have recorded exactly how that data was measured and recorded. Try out different ways of presenting that data, including tables, bar charts and/or line graphs. Finally, analyse and evaluate your data in basic tables, bar charts, line graphs or pie charts.

Key principles of training

The easy way to remember the principles of training is by using the SPORT acronym:

- **S** – specificity
- **PO** – progressive overload
- **R** – reversibility
- **T** – tedium.

Specificity

Specificity within a training programme will vary according to:

- the type of person who is training – it will depend on their initial fitness levels, body type and physiological factors, as well as other individual differences
- the type of activity being trained for – it will depend on the sport itself and the level at which it is to be performed.

Progressive overload

You must build **progressive overload** into a training programme and always bear in mind the following points:

- The levels of general and specific fitness in place at the start of the programme.
- You may have to start very gradually but you must increase the demands as your body adjusts to the work it is doing and the stresses it is experiencing.
- Levels of **plateauing** occur where you progress to a certain level then seem to get stuck there before being able to move on – this can happen more than once.

Progressive overload is linked to the FITT acronym:

- **F** – frequency, or how often training takes place; training more often increases overload.
- **I** – intensity, of how hard you train; extra amounts of activity or increasing weights (if these are being used) increase overload.
- **T** – the time, or duration, of each session; increasing the actual amount of time spent training, or even on one particular aspect of the training, also increases overload.
- **T** – type.

An important factor linked to overload is that of safety. This is why the term progressive overload is often used, because it ensures that the additional demands are added only gradually and safely.

Reversibility

Reversibility will be felt if, for any reason, training either stops or is reduced:

- Positive effects will be lost at roughly the rate of one-third of the time it took to gain them!
- A beginner loses effects at a faster rate than a regular, trained performer.
- Different factors of fitness may be affected in different ways and to different degrees.

Specificity Making training specific to the sport being played/movements used/muscles used/energy system(s) used

Progressive overload Gradual increase in the amount of overload so that fitness gains occur but without potential for injury. Overload is the gradual increase in stress placed on the body during exercise training (more than usual)

Plateauing Where you progress to a certain level then seem to get stuck there before being able to move on

Reversibility Losing fitness levels when you stop exercising

Exam tip

If you get a question about specificity, try to avoid the word 'specific' in your answer. Use words or phrases such as 'most suited to' or 'most appropriate'.

Typical mistake

Overload is often misinterpreted as being a negative factor – as something which can cause damage or injury – when it is exactly the opposite. Used properly and effectively, it is the only way in which to bring about change and improvement.

Exam tip

Remember that overload is a positive aspect and one which is to be encouraged when training. It is not to be confused with 'overuse', which can cause injuries.

Revision activity

Research an elite performer who has been injured to find out how long it took for them to return to the level of fitness they had prior to their injury. Injury is the most common way in which reversibility occurs.

Tedium

Tedium will be experienced if all of the training becomes repetitive for each session, as this is going to have a negative effect and almost certainly prevent progress or **progression**.

Application of the principles of training

Being aware of, and understanding, the principles of training has the following benefits:
- It enables a performer to apply these principles in order to be able to bring about improvements.
- These principles can be applied to particular sports and activities through the first principle of specificity so that they can be 'tailor made' to suit each individual requirement.

Tedium Boredom that can occur from training the same way every time – variety is needed

Progression Gradually and safely increasing the amount of training that you do

Now test yourself

TESTED ☐

1 Which one of the following is the best description of the specificity training principle while weight training?
  a) increasing the weights lifted for each training session
  b) concentrating on training muscles in the upper arm
  c) lifting your maximum weight for one repetition
  d) using all free weights rather than machines. (1 mark)
2 Which one of the following best describes the frequency element of the FITT principle of training?
  a) how hard you exercise
  b) the type of exercise you choose
  c) how much time you take to exercise
  d) how many times a week you exercise. (1 mark)
3 The main training principles are: specificity, progressive overload, reversibility and tedium. Describe *two* of these training principles and give a practical example for each. (6 marks)

There are various types of training. It is important to be aware of the different types and what the particular distinctions are between them.

Circuit training

This type of training consists of a number of different exercises or activities arranged at a circuit. The exercises should be clearly labelled and marked out. When setting out a circuit the following points need to be considered:

- the space that is available
- the equipment available or needed
- the actual number of circuit stations
- the work/rest ratio to be set or used
- the content and demand of the circuit and the ways in which it can be altered
- matching a circuit station to a particular component of fitness.

One of the main **advantages** of circuit training is that it can be adjusted for exercising any part or parts of the body or any muscle group or groups, as well as aerobic or anaerobic fitness. The main **disadvantage** of circuit training is that it is difficult to carry out on your own and that it can take quite a long time to set up and run.

Continuous training

This consists of taking part in sustained exercise at a constant rate (maintaining a steady state) without any rests. This would involve an aerobic demand (see Section 1.4, page 10) for a minimum of twenty minutes (in order to keep the heart and pulse rate high throughout an extended period). Activities commonly used for this type of training include running, swimming, rowing and cycling.

The main **advantage** of continuous training is that it is very easy and quick to set up (it can be undertaken with no specific equipment at all) and that it can be used to target aerobic fitness. The main **disadvantage** is that it is a very specific type of training and therefore not suitable for general training.

Fartlek training

Fartlek is a Swedish word which means 'speed training' and refers to a form of continuous training. It uses a variety of speed, terrain and work/rest ratios. It can often alternate walking, brisk walking, running and fast, steady running. It shares the same advantages and disadvantages as continuous training.

Interval training or high-intensity interval training (HIIT)

HIIT involves periods of exercising hard, interspersed with periods of rest or low-intensity training. It commonly involves running.

The main **advantages** are that it does not require any specialist equipment, it allows individuals to train on their own and it is well suited to anaerobic-type activities. The main **disadvantage** is that it is very specific and not related to general fitness.

> **HIIT** High-intensity interval training, which is an exercise strategy alternating periods of short intense aerobic exercise with less intense recovery periods

> **Typical mistake**
>
> Considering dynamic stretching as an appropriate form of stretching. This is potentially dangerous and harmful if performed incorrectly and can often result in muscle damage and injury.

Static stretching

This is a way to stretch to include flexibility. A stretch is held (an **isometric contraction**) for up to 30 seconds. It is important to ensure that the correct technique is used and to be careful to avoid any overstretching.

The main **advantage** of this is that it can be done anywhere and at any time. The main **disadvantage** is that it concentrates solely one particular component of fitness.

Weight training

Here, a choice can be made about either a weight or an exercise to be used, depending on the fitness aim. The choice could be between strength or **power** training and muscular endurance. When carrying out weight training there is a need to be aware of, and implement, safe practice and lifting techniques. **Spotters** are used to supervise and help.

The main **advantages** of weight training are that it can improve muscle tone, increase muscular endurance, develop muscle size or bulk and assist recovery after injury. The main **disadvantages** are that it requires very specific, specialised, expensive and bulky equipment (which need a lot of space), and to be performed correctly trained spotters can also be required.

Plyometric training

This is training using plyometric exercises such as bounding or depth jumping. It is designed to increase power by using an **eccentric contraction** followed by a larger **concentric contraction**.

The **advantages** of this form of training are that it does not require any specific equipment, it can be undertaken anywhere and it is well suited to a personal training programme. The main **disadvantages** are that it is a very specific form of training and does not help general fitness.

General training considerations

For any of the training methods outlined above it is important to consider the following:
- the training purpose or purposes
- making use of training targets and training zones (see Section 3.5, page 29)
- appropriate use of rest and recovery periods
- matching the type of training to the various fitness needs and to specific sporting activities, for example continuous training would be fully appropriate for marathon runners while plyometric training would be fully appropriate for hurdlers.

> **Isometric contraction**
> A muscle contraction where the length of the muscle does not alter – the contraction is constant, such as pushing against a load
>
> **Power** The product of strength and speed: strength × speed
>
> **Spotters** Assistants in weight training sessions who can help to lower and raise the weights during specific exercises
>
> **Eccentric contraction** Where the tension in the muscle is increased as it lengthens
>
> **Concentric contraction** Where there is increased tension on a muscle as it shortens

> **Exam tip**
>
> Questions on this topic are likely to link to which form of training is most suitable for a specific activity. You also need to be aware of the advantages and disadvantages of each particular form of training.

> **Revision activity**
>
> For each of the training methods outlined in this section, create your own table where you match each training type to a particular sporting activity. In your table state the effect on the body which you would expect that particular type of training to have, and how this makes it the best suited to that activity.

Now test yourself

TESTED ☐

1 All of the following are types of training apart from:
   a) fartlek
   b) plyometric
   c) static stretching
   d) concentric contracting. (1 mark)
2 The most suitable form of training for a marathon runner would be:
   a) weight
   b) circuit
   c) continuous
   d) static stretching. (1 mark)
3 Explain why it is important to vary the order of exercises or stations when carrying out circuit training so that similar activities or exercises do not immediately follow each other. (4 marks)

3.5 Optimising training and injury prevention

It is important to be able to calculate intensities so that you can optimise your training effectively.

Training thresholds

Training thresholds are the actual boundaries of the training zone, which are set out in Figure 12.

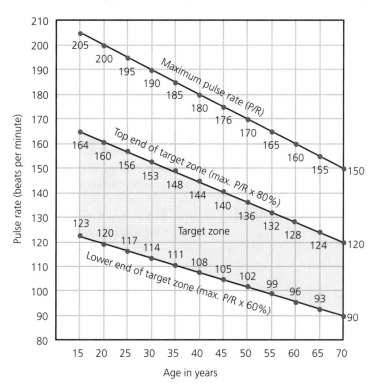

Figure 12 Heart rate training zones.

You can see from Figure 12 that you are able to calculate various aerobic and anaerobic training zones:
- maximal heart rate is 220 minus your age
- the aerobic training zone is 60–80 per cent of maximal heart rate
- the anaerobic training zone is 80–90 per cent of maximal heart rate.

General intensity calculations

In **circuit training** there are three main factors: work time, rest time and actual content. These factors can all be adjusted to determine the fitness aim you are setting out to achieve.

In **weight training** the factors you can adjust to bring about different outcomes are the number of **repetitions (reps)** and **sets**. Another important factor to take into account when weight training is to work out one repetition maximum (**one rep max**), and then calculate how to make use of this with reference to the following:
- **Strength/power training** (high weight/low reps) – should be above 70 per cent of one rep max and approximately three sets of 4–8 reps.
- **Muscular endurance (low weight/high reps)** – should be below 70 per cent of one rep max and approximately three sets of 12–15 reps.

Exam tip

Questions are also likely to link to the requirement within the exam paper to test for 'use of data and data analysis', so it is vital that you understand the calculations above and that you are able to interpret any results obtained. Both of the exam papers state that there may be a question on 'use of data and data analysis', and this is one of the topics which requires the use of calculations. It is for this reason that you should be familiar with the three factors above and be confident about your ability to accurately calculate all three. This is why you must remember to take your calculator into both exams too!

Repetitions (reps)
The number of times you move the weights when training. If using barbells then one barbell curl would equal one repetition

Sets The number of repetitions (reps) you carry out for a particular weight activity without stopping. So each time you complete your repetitions of the barbell curl you have completed one set

One rep max The maximal amount that can be lifted in one repetition by a muscle or group of muscles, with the correct technique. So, for your barbell curl this would be the maximum barbell weight you are able to curl using the correct technique

Considerations to prevent injury

As a general rule, the training type and intensity should always match the training purpose. For example, you need to consider whether you are focusing on aerobic or anaerobic exercise and choose the appropriate training type and intensity accordingly.

The following factors should always be taken into account (where applicable) in order to prevent injury:

- a warm-up should be completed (see Section 3.6, page 32)
- overtraining needs to be avoided, therefore it would be important to select the appropriate weight
- appropriate clothing and footwear should be worn
- taping or bracing should be used as necessary
- hydration should be maintained, so taking on fluids is essential
- when stretching you should not overstretch or bounce
- correct technique **must** be used at all times; this is particularly important with any lifting and/or lowering techniques
- there must be appropriate rest between sessions in order to allow for recovery.

Now test yourself

TESTED ☐

1 Using the correct calculation, work out what the maximum heart rate would be for a fifteen year old. (3 marks)
2 The aerobic training zone is:
   a) 70–90 per cent of maximal heart rate
   b) 60–80 per cent of maximal heart rate
   c) 80–90 per cent of maximal heart rate
   d) 60–70 per cent of maximal heart rate. (1 mark)
3 Using examples, explain the difference between repetitions and sets. (4 marks)
4 Explain why you should avoid overstretching or bouncing when performing stretching exercises. (3 marks)

Revision activity

The best way for you to understand the key terms above is to take part in some actual training sessions using weights. You should calculate your own one rep max for a specific muscle or group of muscles, and try out the two main variations of reps and sets to gain a better understanding. You could even generate and collect some data to analyse.

Typical mistake

To be aware of, and perform, warm-ups consistently but not to forget about the need for a cool-down as well to also help prevent injury!

3.6 Training techniques and effective warm-up and cool-down

It is important to be aware of **training techniques**, as distinct from training types.

High-altitude training

This is used as a technique for aerobic training and it is carried out in the following way:

- Training takes place at a high altitude. This is usually a geographical area of land which is over 2000 m above sea level, where there is less oxygen.
- The body adapts by making more red blood cells to carry oxygen.
- This additional oxygen-carrying capacity of the red blood cells becomes an advantage for endurance athletes when they return to sea level to compete.

There are real benefits to be gained for some performers by taking part in high-altitude training as there can be some very positive short-term advantages. However, the effects do diminish quite quickly. There are practical disadvantages involved too; as there are only limited geographical areas where this is possible, it is time consuming and therefore expensive in terms of travel and accommodation.

> **Typical mistake**
>
> It is important not to confuse the term seasonal aspects with the seasons of the year.

Endurance runners often train at high altitudes to gain a competitive advantage. They arrange this to take place just as their pre-season training is ending and their competition phase is about to start.

Seasonal aspects

The training seasons are:
- **Pre-season** (also known as preparation) – this is where the emphasis is on preparation for the playing season to come. The aims the performer has at this time are to concentrate on general (possible aerobic) and specific fitness needs and requirements. In a sport such as professional football, the performers often attend pre-season training camps that start with light training sessions which are then gradually increased in intensity.
- **Competition season** (also known as peak/playing season) – this is where the emphasis is on maintaining fitness levels and working on specific skills needed for the best possible playing performance. In a sport such as rugby, the performers would not only be maintaining high fitness levels for each match but also be working on practising particular set moves and drills – often taking into account the strengths and weaknesses of the next opponents for each match or game.
- **Post-season** (also known as transition) – the emphasis here is on effective rest and light aerobic exercise to maintain a level of general fitness.

Warming up and cooling down

Ensuring that a correct and appropriate warm-up and cool-down takes place should be an essential aspect for every occasion when physical activity takes place. It is an essential preparation and failing to do so often results in injury.

Warming up

An effective warm-up should include the following:
- gradual pulse-raising activities
- stretching
- skill-based practices and/or activity familiarisation
- mental preparation
- activity to increase the amount of oxygen to the working muscles.

The benefits of an effective warm-up include:
- effectively gradually increasing the body temperature
- increasing the range of movement possible
- gradually increasing the amount of effort to the full pace required
- providing effective psychological preparation
- enabling practice of movement skills through the whole range of movement
- reducing the likelihood or the possibility of injury.

Cooling down

An effective cool-down should include the following:
- continuing to maintain elevated breathing and heart rate through reducing activity to a jog or walk
- gradually reducing the intensity of the activity or exercise
- carrying out general stretching.

The benefits of an effective cool-down include:
- allowing the body to recover from the intensive exercise preceding this phase
- the removal of lactic acid, carbon dioxide and waste products
- helping to prevent delayed onset muscle soreness (**DOMS**).

> **Exam tip**
> Questions relating to seasonal aspects are likely to focus on you being able to both apply and justify the characteristics of a particular sporting activity in relation to the three 'seasons' outlined opposite. Remember these are not the seasons of spring, summer, autumn, winter!

> **Revision activity**
> For one of the three non-examined assessment activities you are likely to be assessed on researching the seasonal aspects and preparations that an elite performer would carry out for their particular sporting activity.

> **Typical mistake**
> Not making a warm-up specific to the sport or activity about to take place. A gymnast would concentrate on effective and relevant stretches as a priority and a games player would place greater emphasis on pulse raisers.

> **Exam tip**
> Questions relating to both the warm-up and cool-down are likely to focus on what would be appropriate for a particular sporting activity. You should be able to describe an activity-specific warm-up and cool-down that you used for one of your three non-examined assessment activities.

> **DOMS** Delayed onset muscle soreness

Now test yourself

1 All of the following are true about high-altitude training apart from:
   a) it needs to be carried out at over 2000 m above sea level
   b) the benefits gained from using this technique are relatively long term
   c) it increases the number of red blood cells for oxygen-carrying capacity
   d) there is less oxygen in the air at high altitude. (1 mark)
2 An effective warm-up should include all of the following except:
   a) a slow walk or jog
   b) stretching
   c) skill-based practices
   d) mental preparation. (1 mark)
3 Describe, in full, three benefits to be gained by a performer by carrying out an effective cool-down. (6 marks)

Summary

This chapter concentrates on developing your knowledge and understanding of the principles of training and different training methods in order to plan, carry out, monitor and evaluate personal exercise and training programmes.

The main areas for you to review, revise and be aware of are as follows:
- The relationship between health and fitness.
- The components of fitness.
- Being able to link sports and physical activity to the required components of fitness.
- The reasons for fitness testing.
- The possible limitations which can exist in fitness testing.
- Being able to measure the components of fitness with specific tests for each separate component.
- Being aware of the testing procedures and organisation required for each specific fitness component test.
- Being able to demonstrate how the data is collected for each of the different tests, including being aware of how test scores are measured and recorded.
- Being able to present the data which has been collected in tables using bar charts and/or line graphs.
- Being able to analyse and evaluate data which has been collected in basic tables, bar charts, line graphs or pie charts.
- Understanding the key principles of training and overload.
- Being able to apply the principles of training to sporting examples.
- Understanding the different types of training and being aware of the distinctions between them.
- Being able to identify the advantages and disadvantages of each type of training method.
- Being aware of how to optimise training and prevent injury.
- Understanding specific training techniques – such as high-altitude training as a form of aerobic training.
- Understanding the seasonal aspects of training.
- Understanding the importance of the effective use of a warm-up and cool-down.

4 Sports psychology

4.1 Classification of skills

This chapter focuses on psychological factors that can affect performers in physical activity and sport.

Skill and ability

These two terms link together very closely and it is important to understand, and be able to apply, the definitions for each of them:
- **Skills** – learned actions or learned behaviours with the intention of bringing about predetermined results with maximum certainty and the minimum outlay of time and energy.
- **Ability** – **inherited**, stable **traits** that determine an individual's potential to learn or acquire a skill.

Classification of skills

Skills are broken down into groups. You need to know about the following four categories:
- **Basic/complex** – these range from a very **basic** skill such as walking/ jogging and jumping/throwing to far more **complex** and difficult skills such as the pole vault.
- **Open/closed** – an **open skill** is a skill which is performed in a certain way to deal with a changing or unstable environment (such as outwitting an opponent). A **closed skill** is one which is not affected by the environment of performers within it, as the skill tends to be performed the same way each time. A footballer taking part in a match is in a constantly changing environment and they may have to change or adapt their skills according to the demands of the game (therefore open skills). A trampolinist, on the other hand, is performing in an environment that does not change as the equipment used is always the same (therefore closed skills). These examples are two extreme ends of a **skills continuum**.
- **Self-paced/externally paced** – a **self-paced skill** is one which is started when the performer decides to start it (the speed, rate or pace of the skill is controlled by the performer). An example of this is serving in tennis, as you would decide when and where to throw the ball up, when to make contact and where to aim it. An **externally paced skill** is one where the skill is started by an external factor (the speed, rate or pace of the skill is controlled by external factors such as an opponent), so receiving the ball from a tennis serve would be started by your opponent serving to you.
- **Gross/fine** – a **gross** movement (required for a gross skill) is where you use large muscle groups to perform big, strong powerful movements, such as a lay-up shot in basketball. A **fine** movement (required for fine skills) is a small and precise movement, showing high levels of accuracy and co-ordination, and it involves the use of a small group of muscles, such as a delicate net drop volley in doubles tennis.

> **Inherited** Properties or genetic qualities received from parents
>
> **Trait** A distinguishing characteristic or quality of a personal nature
>
> **Skills continuum** A continuous sequence where the most basic and simple skills are at one end and the more complex and difficult ones are at the other, extreme, end

> **Exam tip**
>
> Be aware that performers often avoid setting outcome goals as they rely on factors which they (the performer) cannot control, such as other performers. Therefore, beginners prefer to avoid them as winning could well be an unrealistic goal and failure can result in being demotivated.

The server will be using self-paced skills as they serve, and the receiver will be using externally paced skills when reacting to the serve received and completing the return of serve.

Goal setting

When considering goal setting it is important to first consider the different goal types that are possible. These are:

- **Performance goals** – these are personal standards to be achieved. This type of goal is where performers compare themselves against what they have already done, or suggests what they are going to do. There is no comparison with other performers.
- **Outcome goals** – these are where the focus is on the end result, such as winning.

SMART targets

This is a method of goal setting used to improve or optimise performance under the following headings:

- **Specific** – the goal must be specific to the demands of the sport, the muscles used or the movements used.
- **Measurable** – it must be possible to measure whether the goals set have been met.
- **Accepted** – these goals must be accepted by the performer and any others involved in setting the goals, such as a coach or teacher.
- **Realistic** – the goals must actually be possible to complete or achieve.
- **Time-bound** – a set period of time must be imposed.

Revision activity

Make a note of your own person goal setting against the two headings. The performance goal (the standard which you were able to achieve) can be the results of one of the tests which you carried out in Section 3.2, page 22. The outcome goal (an example of the end result, such as whether you won or not) can be linked to one of your non-examined assessment activities you have undertaken when you competed against an opponent.

Revision activity

Consider the information about performance goals and use the SMART target acronym to improve or optimise a performance you have undertaken while studying the GCSE PE course.

Now test yourself

TESTED

1. All of the following are classifications of skill apart from:
   a) complex
   b) closed
   c) motor
   d) gross. (1 mark)
2. SMART targets include all of the following except:
   a) specific
   b) attainable
   c) measurable
   d) realistic. (1 mark)
3. Explain the difference between a self-paced skill and an externally paced skill in a named physical activity. (6 marks)

4.2 Basic information processing

Information processing is about making decisions. It involves gathering data for the **display** (this means your senses) and prioritising the most important **stimuli** to make a suitable decision.

Basic information processing model

Each stage of this information processing model has a particular role:

- **Input** – this is what has been received from the **senses** (sight, hearing and touch). The performer makes use of selective attention, whereby they are able to prioritise which specific parts of the input they have received are the most important and relevant.
- **Decision making** – this is where the performer has to make the appropriate choice or response from their memory. This could be their short-term memory, which is retained for about 30 seconds, or their long-term memory, which can stretch back over a far longer period of months or even years.
- **Output** – this is where the information that has already been processed is sent to the muscles in order to be able to carry out the selected and desired response.
- **Feedback** – this can be received by the performer themselves (**intrinsic feedback**) and/or from others (**extrinsic feedback**) such as a teacher or coach.

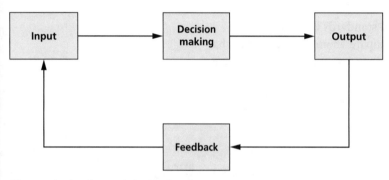

Figure 1 Basic model of information processing.

Guidance and information on feedback

When a coach, teacher or learner is considering giving feedback they should try to consider which types of **guidance** would be best suited to beginners and elite performers. The types of guidance that can be given are:

- **Visual** – this involves being the performer being able to actually see something, using the sense of sight, so this could be a demonstration, a video or YouTube clip, or photographs.
- **Verbal** – this involves using your sense of hearing and could be as simple as listening to someone giving instructions.
- **Manual** – this is where a performer could actually be assisted in a physical movement. Supporting someone doing a gymnastic vault is a very common example of this.
- **Mechanical** – this involves the use of objects or aids. An example of this is the RoboGolfPro machine which professional golfers use and which physically guides the player through a perfect swing.

Display Being made aware of mentally via your senses

Stimuli Things that arouse activity or energy in someone

Senses These are all connected to the nervous system, and are sight (vision), hearing, taste, smell and touch. Sight, hearing and touch are the main senses which would be associated with performing physical activities

Feedback Information a performer receives about their performance

Intrinsic feedback Sensations that were felt by the performer, providing information from movement received via receptors in the muscles. This is also known as kinaesthetic feedback

Extrinsic feedback Received from outside the performer, such as from a teacher or coach

Guidance A method to convey information to a performer

Exam tip

You may well be asked to draw the boxes in Figure 1 and to explain the stages of the basic information processing model using actual sporting examples.

Types of feedback

There are several types of feedback that are suitable for different levels of performer (beginner or elite). These include:

- **Positive/negative** – this is as straightforward as being able to tell the performer what was good and correct about the performance (positive), and what was bad or incorrect about the performance (negative).
- **Knowledge of results** – this is the feedback the performer gets through the end result of their performance, or by being told by an observer at the end of the performance.
- **Knowledge of performance** – this is how the performer feels about their actions from the performance that has just taken place.
- **Extrinsic/intrinsic feedback** – either from themselves (intrinsic) or from others (extrinsic).

Revision activity

Draw your own version of Figure 1 and link it to an actual sporting activity or situation, filling in each box with the relevant information. Try to use an actual situation that you have experienced and explain, in your own words, how you processed the information for each heading.

Revision activity

Research, through the internet, the RoboGolfPro to see a video showing how mechanical guidance can be used to improve a golfer's swing.

Exam tip

You are likely to be asked questions relating to choosing and justifying which types of feedback (outlined here) are most appropriate for beginners and elite performers.

Now test yourself

TESTED ☐

1. All of the following are types of guidance apart from:
   a) extrinsic
   b) verbal
   c) visual
   d) mechanical. (1 mark)
2. Types of feedback include all of the following except:
   a) negative
   b) supportive
   c) positive
   d) knowledge of results. (1 mark)
3. Describe the types of guidance you would be most likely to recommend to be used by an elite gymnastic performer. (6 marks)

4.3 Mental preparation for performance

Arousal

A performer needs the correct level of **arousal** in order to be fully mentally prepared for a performance.

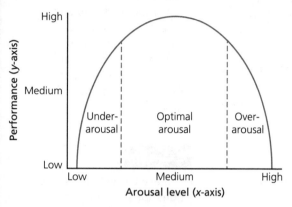

Figure 2 The inverted U theory.

You can see from Figure 2 where the performance level (y-axis) and the arousal level (x-axis) both move from high to low with the best possible performance (also known as the optimum level of arousal) at the mid-point on the graph. When the performance level (on the y-axis) and the arousal level (on the x-axis) are at the highest point of the curve, the best possible performance is then possible – this is known as the optimum level of arousal.

There are two particular states of readiness you need to be aware of in relation to this:

- **Under-arousal** – performance levels are likely to be low (as shown on the graph).
- **Over-arousal** – performance levels are also likely to be low (as shown on the graph).

In addition to the two extreme states of readiness, it is important to be aware of the link between optimum arousal levels and specific skills being performed in a physical activity or sport:

- **Gross movement skills** require higher levels of arousal. The performer needs to be very alert in order to be able to make use of strength, endurance or speed which might be required to perform the big or strong movements in sporting actions.
- **Fine movement skills** require lower levels of arousal. The mind and body need to be calm in order for the levels of co-ordination and concentration to be at the required level for the small, precise movements involved in the sporting actions.

Arousal A physical and mental (physiological and psychological) state of alertness or readiness, varying from deep sleep to intense excitement or alertness

Gross movement skills Involve large muscle groups combining to perform big, strong, powerful movements

Fine movement skills Small and precise movements that require high levels of accuracy and co-ordination

---

Revision activity

Practise drawing Figure 2 on your own and labelling it exactly as shown. This is specifically noted as a task you must be able to complete.

Exam tip

You are likely to be asked questions linking appropriate arousal levels to specific skills, rather than the sports or activities. Avoid just stating a sport. For example, a successful tackle in rugby will need a high arousal level but the game, or sport, or rugby in itself would not require this.

Stress management

It is crucial to be aware of the importance of arousal and also to be aware of the need to be able to control the levels which may be required through the effective use of **stress** management. These techniques can be applied before or during a sporting performance, and include the following:

- **Deep breathing** – if the performer becomes very aroused their breathing can become rapid and erratic. By using deep-breathing techniques and taking slow, deep breaths the breathing can be returned to normal as the supply of oxygen to the brain increases.
- **Mental rehearsal, visualisation and imagery** – this requires the performer to change the way they think in order to change the way they behave. These changes must be aimed at making the performer more relaxed and calm, so the mental rehearsal could be going over a previously successful action or performance, the visualisation and imagery recalling or imagining a positive outcome. These techniques would need to be carried out before a sporting performance.
- **Positive self-talk** – this involves you mentally reflecting and 'reframing' your thoughts, making sure that any negative thoughts are replaced by more positive ones. For example, if you have just played a bad shot in a tennis rally and lost the point, 'reframe' in order to consider how you could have selected a more appropriate shot.

> **Stress** Physical, mental or emotional strain or tension
>
> **Mental rehearsal, visualisation and imagery** Cognitive relaxation techniques involving control of mental thoughts and imagining positive outcomes
>
> **Positive self-talk** Developing cognitive positive thoughts about your own performance
>
> **Cognitive** Relating to the mental processes of perception, memory, judgement and reasoning

Now test yourself

TESTED

1 All of the following require high levels of arousal apart from:
   a) a rugby tackle
   b) sprinting 100 m
   c) throwing a dart
   d) throwing a javelin. (1 mark)
2 Effective stress management includes all of the following except:
   a) an effective warm-up
   b) deep breathing
   c) mental rehearsal
   d) positive self-talk. (1 mark)
3 Explain why both over-arousal and under-arousal can result in low performance levels. (6 marks)

> **Revision activity**
>
> You need to be aware of arousal levels required in all sporting activities which you take part in. Keep a log of the levels of arousal which you need in activities you regularly take part in and see if you can make use of any, or all, of the stress management techniques. Make a note of which of the techniques you use are most successful and describe why and how they were successful.

4.4 Aggression, personality types and motivation

Aggression

Aggression is commonly used in sporting activities in two particular ways:

● **Direct aggression** – this is aimed directly at another player or performer and it involves some form of physical contact. Direct aggression is often very closely linked to the rules of an activity; for example, punching is clearly allowed in the rules in boxing but not in football, and a full body tackle is allowed in rugby but not in football.

● **Indirect aggression** – this is aggression which does not involve any physical contact. The aggression is taken out on an object to gain advantage, such as hitting a tennis ball harder, which is effectively taking out the aggression on the ball. Indirect aggression is allowed within the rules of sporting activities.

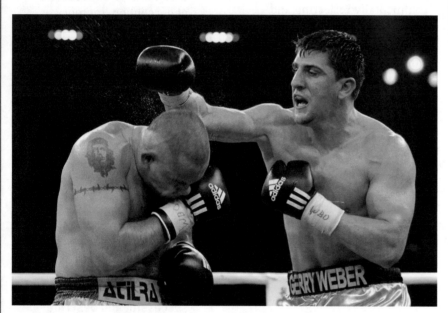

Boxing is a sport which specifically encourages direct aggression as a knock-out wins a boxing contest.

Personality types

There are two identified personality types: **introvert** and **extrovert**. Both types have specific characteristics associated with them:

● **Introverts** are shy, quiet and thoughtful individuals who enjoy being on their own and are often described as being 'loners'. These types of individuals tend to play individual sports where concentration and precision (fine skills) are required, which is linked to having low arousal levels.

● **Extroverts** enjoy interacting with others, are sociable and are aroused by others. They tend to be enthusiastic and talkative and are prone to boredom if they are left isolated or on their own. These types of individuals tend to play team sports where there is a faster pace to the play, concentration levels can be lower and gross skills are commonly used.

Aggression A deliberate intent to harm or injure another person, which can be physical or mental

Introvert A quiet, passive, reserved, shy personality type, usually associated with individual sports performance

Extrovert A sociable, active, talkative, outgoing personality type, usually associated with team sports players

Revision activity

Go through the list of the team and individual activities which are available in the non-examination assessment and try to match each activity up to one of the two personality types. You might find it quite a challenge when you consider some of the positional choices in some sports and the variety of activities possible in athletics.

Exam tip

Questions are likely to ask you to link a particular personality type with a particular sporting activity or role, and also to justify why you think this is the case.

Motivation

Motivation is the drive to succeed or the desire (want) to achieve something or to be inspired to do something. There are two distinct types of motivation:

- **Intrinsic** – this is the drive from within, such as for pride, satisfaction, a sense of accomplishment or self-worth. A performer may get a real sense of personal achievement and self-satisfaction. Runners who are able to beat previous personal bests or golfers who are able to reduce their handicaps are two examples of performers attaining intrinsic motivation.
- **Extrinsic** – this is the drive to perform well or to win in order to gain external rewards such as prizes, trophies or money. Extrinsic motivation is the drive experienced by a performer when striving to achieve a reward. This external reward is provided by an outside source such as another person. It can be **tangible** if it takes the form of a certificate, medal or trophy, but it can also be **intangible** if it takes the form of feedback, praise or even applause from a crowd or an audience.

Both intrinsic motivation and extrinsic motivation have their own particular merits:

- Intrinsic motivation is generally deemed to be more effective, so it is more commonly used.
- The overuse of extrinsic motivation can undermine the benefits of using intrinsic motivation. In many contests, only one person can be the winner so the majority of competitors end up being losers and therefore lose motivation.
- A performer can become reliant on extrinsic motivation and not want to compete without some sort of reward being available.
- Intrinsic motivation is more likely to lead to continued effort and participation.
- Extrinsic rewards can also result in feelings of pride and self-satisfaction.

> **Revision activity**
>
> Try to list the number of times you have experienced intrinsic and extrinsic motivation in the last year of sporting performances.

> **Tangible** Real or actual, capable of being touched as it has an actual physical presence
>
> **Intangible** Incapable of being perceived by the sense of touch or of being grasped, and not having a physical presence

> **Exam tip**
>
> Questions relating to both intrinsic and extrinsic motivation are likely to focus on being able to evaluate the specific merits which each type of motivation has. This would then often be linked to actual sporting examples.

Now test yourself

TESTED ☐

1 All of the following are characteristics of an introvert apart from:
  a) talkative
  b) shy
  c) quiet
  d) thoughtful. (1 mark)
2 Extrinsic motivation includes all of the following except:
  a) trophies
  b) praise
  c) feedback
  d) pride. (1 mark)
3 Explain why intrinsic motivation may be more suitable to a beginner in sport rather than an elite performer. (6 marks)

Summary

This chapter concentrates on developing your knowledge and understanding of the psychological factors that can affect performers in physical activity and sport.

The main areas for you to review, revise and be aware of are as follows:

- Skill and ability – definitions regarding what these are.
- The classifications of skills – including the definitions of these different classifications and how to choose and justify the appropriate classifications in relation to sporting examples.
- Definitions of the different types of goals and the appropriate performance and/or outcome targets for sporting examples.
- The use and evaluation of goal setting to improve and/or optimise performance.
- The effective use of SMART targets to improve and/or optimise performance.
- Understanding a basic information processing model and the role of each stage, and then being able to apply this basic information processing model to skills from specific sporting examples.
- The types of guidance which are available for performers – notably beginners and elite-level performers. This includes what would be appropriate for each type of performer as well as being aware of examples of how this guidance could be given.

- The types of feedback available which can be given to beginners and elite performers. This includes being able to identify examples and evaluate the effectiveness of these different types of feedback.
- Mental preparation for performance – being able to understand and define arousal.
- What the inverted U theory is and specifically being able to both draw and appropriately label the graph.
- How optimal arousal levels can vary according to the skills being performed in different physical activities or sport.
- How it is possible to control arousal using stress management techniques before or during a sporting performance.
- Understanding the difference between direct and indirect aggression, and being able to apply this to specific sporting examples.
- Understanding the differences between an extrovert and introvert personality type, and being able to give examples of sports which suit these personality types.
- Being able to define intrinsic and extrinsic motivation and explain appropriate examples linked to sporting examples.
- Being able to evaluate the merits of intrinsic and extrinsic motivation in sport.

5a Socio-cultural influences

5.1 Engagement patterns of different social groups

REVISED

The levels of engagement (which effectively means levels of participation) in physical activity and sport can differ between different social groups. Set patterns are often established within these groups, which are considered below.

Gender

The body shapes, physiques and sizes of men and women (and therefore **metabolism**) are generally different. Women tend to be smaller and have a flatter, broader pelvis and smaller heart and lungs:

- Women have more body fat – up to 30 per cent more.
- On average, women have two-thirds the strength of men, with less total muscle mass. This clearly disadvantages women in strength-based events.
- Levels of flexibility tend to be greater in females, often helped by having less muscle mass.
- Boys tend to overtake girls in terms of height, weight and strength from about the age of eleven. This is one of the reasons why single-sex sport tends to start being practised from this age onwards.

> **Metabolism** The biochemical processes that happen in the body and keep us alive

Perceived differences

The physical differences related to gender are clear. However, this does not mean that either gender is particularly advantaged or disadvantaged: both may have advantages and disadvantages in all sports. At one time some sports were only considered to be suitable for one sex (netball for women and football for men, for example), but this is not the case now. Women were discriminated against in the past and not allowed to take part in some events and activities but there are equal opportunities in place now.

Race, religion and culture

These three are very closely linked in the following ways:

- People's cultural attitudes change over time. For example, until quite recently there was a lot of opposition to women's boxing in the UK. Some religions have single-sex rules that can prevent women from taking part in mixed-sex sport activities.
- Many traditions also have dress codes, which particularly relate to what women are required to wear. In sport, this can especially apply to swimming, where religious rules forbid the wearing of swimming costumes if men are present.
- Religious dress codes can also involve the head and hair. For instance, the Sikh religion requires that men wear a turban (sometimes a smaller version of the turban, called a *patka*). This could potentially cause problems in some activities; for example, if a safety helmet was also required or in swimming activities.

- Some religions also have dietary guidelines that could affect training and competition. For example, Muslims fast during Ramadan. Guidelines may also be in place that forbid taking part on certain days. For example, in Judaism and in Christianity there are rules about keeping one day a week as a special day for prayer and family.

Age

Age is a factor that people have no control over. It is also a **physiological factor**, as there are various physical effects which ageing has on the body. These effects can then influence levels of participation in physical activities. Examples include:

- Very young children cannot cope with difficult tasks, which can affect their ability to learn and practise. This is why some sports are not introduced until children are older.
- Flexibility decreases with age and therefore makes some activities, such as gymnastics, more difficult as you get older.
- Oxygen capacity and reaction time decrease as you get older.
- Injury and disease become more common as you get older; bones can become more brittle and recovery times are longer.
- Skill levels start to increase as you get into your teens and twenties but may then start to decline as you get older.
- Strength, like skill, starts to increase as you get older, peaking in the twenties and thirties but then decreasing as you enter your forties.

> **Physiological factor** A factor that affects your living body and therefore affects you physically

> **Exam tip**
>
> Remember that the particular age of a participant can be an advantage *or* a disadvantage – often depending on the type of activity undertaken.

Some activities clearly get more difficult as you get older!

Age divisions

Because age can be such a deciding factor for the majority of sports, especially for younger people, participation is usually divided up into set categories. In school this is usually organised as year groups, but sports and governing bodies also organise competitions into particular age groups such as under fourteens, under sixteens and under eighteens. This still allows a particularly gifted young performer to take part in a category above their age but does not allow for an older performer to drop down any age categories.

> **Exam tip**
>
> It is important to know why age divisions are put in place – these all link to the physiological factors identified in this topic.

Family, friends and peers

The three groups of family, friends and peers all have both positive and negative influences on engagement patterns:

- **Positive** – parents, friends and **peers** may encourage you to participate and even join in with you. Many sporting activities are quite expensive to take part in due to the costs of equipment, training and transport, so parents who are able, and willing, to pay for this are clearly helping to raise the engagement levels.
- **Negative** – if your parents, friends and peers do not see the positive benefits of being engaged in participation they are likely to try to put you off. This can particularly be the case with peer pressure, and 'anti-sport' groups of friends can be very influential in making you conform to their beliefs.

Disability

Disability can be physical or mental. It can also be permanent or temporary. Physical activities are now organised very efficiently to take into account the factor of disability. For example:

- **Adapted activities** – there is a huge range of ways in which activities are adapted to allow disabled people to participate. For example, wheelchair rugby, which has specific rules relating to how the wheelchairs themselves can be used in physical contact.
- **Adapted equipment** – such as the footballs used by blind footballers that have ball bearings inside the ball, which the players can hear as the ball moves.
- **Disability classifications** – these ensure that disabled competitors are able to compete with others who have the same, or a very similar, disability, so making the competition fairer.
- **Provision for disabled people** – this includes making sure that car parks have designated wider parking bays, ramp access for wheelchairs, disabled lifts, automatic doors, special changing areas and toilets, wider corridors, and so on.

Disabled sports are now recognised as separate categories of sport in their own right. Today, there is much less discrimination against disabled participants than there used to be.

Common engagement pattern factors

All of the factors listed below can link significantly to the engagement patterns of the social groups listed above:

- **Attitudes** – these can be both positive and negative and are very closely linked to the effect of peer pressure in particular.
- **Role models** – these are very important and can exist in any of the groups listed above. There is a great deal of responsibility on role models (especially professional sports performers) to set good examples for others to follow.
- **Accessibility** – this is related to your ability to be able to access the opportunities available and can include finding, and getting to, the correct and appropriate facilities as well as accessing clubs and activities you wish to engage in. This is particularly relevant to disabled participants.
- **Media coverage** (see Section 5.2, page 51) – the **media** can help to make particular activities popular (if there is wide coverage of them) or unpopular (if there is little or no coverage or bad publicity).

> **Exam tip**
>
> Questions relating to the influence of family, friends and peers tend to relate to the positive and negative effects they can have.

> **Peers** People who are equal to you in terms of age, background and social status
>
> **Media** Diversified technologies which include printed material, broadcasting, social networks and advertising

> **Exam tip**
>
> The examiner may ask how disabled people are catered for as particular types of participants, and also how sports and competitions are organised for them.

- **Sexism** and **stereotyping** – these most commonly refer to females but there can be examples where they apply equally to males as well.
- **Family commitments** – a family (particularly a large one) may not be able to make the required commitments. Work may be a priority and the financial implications may be too high.
- **Available leisure time** – this can link to the leisure time you have, as well as that of family, friends and peers. School and work will tend to take up a majority of the time available.
- **Familiarity** – a 'new' or different activity may lack the appeal of a more traditional one.
- **Education** – not all cultures have the advantages which are gained by a comprehensive and free education system, so may not know about the real health, fitness and well-being benefits of regularly engaging in physical activity (see Chapter 6).
- **Socio-economic factors and disposable income** – these factors can include levels of housing (living conditions) and care and also the amount of money that might be available after all essential bills and commitments have been met.

Adaptability and inclusiveness

It is the aim of all schools in the UK that the curriculum is inclusive. This means that you should have the opportunity to try out any physical activity you would like. Many clubs and sports have the same **adaptable** approach.

By adapting sports from mainstream versions, or designing new sports, people with limited access (disability or limited income, for example) can participate more easily. In this way, more activities can be made to be more inclusive. Some sports can be adapted to enable wheelchair users to participate, for example wheelchair basketball.

> **Sexism** Attitudes or behaviour based on traditional stereotypes of gender roles
>
> **Stereotyping** An oversimplified perception or generalisation about a group of people
>
> **Leisure time** When you are free to choose what you do; this is usually the time after work or school
>
> **Adaptable** Having the potential to change with ease

> **Typical mistake**
>
> The idea that stereotyping and sexism only apply to females. They can also apply to males.

> **Revision activity**
>
> Carry out a survey of the different leisure provisions which are provided in your area to enable people to make the best use of their available leisure time. See if you can also categorise the specific social groups the leisure activity is targeting and focusing on.

Now test yourself

TESTED ☐

1 Which one of the following shows the effects of gender on participation in physical activity?
   a) females have lower levels of concentration than males in physical activities
   b) males feel more pain than females in physical activities
   c) males are generally stronger than females
   d) females are less likely to show high skill levels in physical activities. (1 mark)
2 Explain why the majority of sports become single sex as males and females get older. (4 marks)
3 Describe the ways in which the culture of a particular society might influence certain levels of participation in physical activities. (4 marks)
4 Which of the following is *not* likely to decrease as you get older?
   a) strength
   b) oxygen capacity
   c) learning ability
   d) reaction time. (1 mark)
5 Explain why age divisions are commonly used in competitive sport and give an example. (4 marks)
6 Give four ways that physical activities are now organised more efficiently to take into account the factor of disability. (4 marks)

5b Commercialisation of physical activity and sport

5.2 Sponsorship

REVISED

There is a very close relationship between sport, sponsorship and the media.

Types of sponsorship

Sponsorship: range and scope

Sponsorship has an effect on sport at just about all levels.

Specific sports and competitions

Many sports arrange and negotiate sponsorship deals, and the sponsors like the opportunity to be associated with a high-profile and successful sport. For example, in professional football, the Premier League has one sponsor, the Football League has another, and the two major cup competitions (FA Cup and 'League Cup') also have sponsors.

Teams and events

National teams and major clubs have their own sponsors. As this is the highest level of sport there is usually no shortage of companies and organisations willing to pay for this privilege. There will be a great number of willing sponsors for many high-profile international events. For example, for the London Olympic Games in 2012, Adidas sponsored the team and supplied kit (this caused a clash with Nike who had individual kit deals with athletes) while Coca-Cola was the main event sponsor.

Every Premier League and football league club has a sponsor logo on its team shirt and this can often vary from year to year. Many of these clubs are now increasingly having their venues or stadiums renamed after their sponsors. For example, the Oval cricket ground has changed its name four times in recent years from 'The Kennington' to 'The Fosters' to 'The Brit' and then 'The Kia Oval' in December 2010 for a deal worth £3.5 million over a five-year period.

Individuals

High-profile sports performers are able to negotiate their own personal sponsorships. The higher the profile of the performer, the greater the amount of the sponsorship. For example, after he became the world number one golfer in 2012, Rory McIlroy signed a ten-year deal with Nike guaranteeing him £155 million (which works out at £420,000 a day). In 1999, footballer David Beckham signed a lifetime deal with Adidas worth £100 million. In 2017, footballer Cristiano Ronaldo revealed that he earns £191 million a year (that works out at £520,000 a day!) and about 90 per cent of those earnings are from business and sponsorship deals. However, these huge deals are only available for the highest profile performers. It is much more difficult to obtain sponsorship for lower profile sports and performers.

> **Commercialisation**
> Managing or exploiting (an organisation or activity) in a way designed to make a profit
>
> **Commercialised activity**
> Sponsorship and the media only

> **Revision activity**
>
> Sponsorship deals are constantly changing and being renegotiated, so research some of the more recent sponsorship deals which have been negotiated since the time you started on your GCSE PE course.

Acceptability of sponsorship

Not all companies or brands are acceptable to the authorities who set the rules for specific sports. Tobacco and any smoking products have now been banned for many years after once being very prominent in many sports.

Alcoholic drinks are not acceptable in many sports; this is especially the case if the sports are particularly associated with younger performers.

Some foods, especially from some fast-food chains, have been deemed unacceptable due to disputes over the nutritional value of their products. This controversy has even affected some soft drinks manufacturers, who have made efforts to reduce sugar levels in their products as a result.

Recently, there has been controversy about financial loan companies and betting firms as some people think these companies encourage people to get into debt or to waste money that they need for more important things. For example, Newcastle United footballer Papiss Cissé objected to wearing his club shirt advertising Wonga (a loan company) for this reason (although he later changed his mind). Also, some performers have refused to wear the advertising logos (or blacked them out) on religious grounds.

A photo of Leicester City player Shinji Okazaki is used in an advertisement inside this department store in Thailand.

Types of sponsorship

- **Money payments (financial)** – this is the most common form of sponsorship. It involves the sponsors paying an agreed fee in return for which the individual, club or team joins in advertising campaigns for the sponsor's product and regularly uses the product.
- **Equipment** – the sponsor provides all the equipment a performer needs, usually the brand of the sponsor. Some brands even design and promote a range of equipment using the performer's name.
- **Clothing** – as with equipment, all the performer's clothing and footwear is provided so that the brand name is given a high profile. This is one of the most competitive areas of sponsorship because of the size of the sports clothing and footwear industry.
- **Accessories** – performers are paid to wear items ranging from watches (worn by tennis players, often on the serving-arm wrist so that it is seen by cameras) to sunglasses (standard for cricketers) and hats. Performers even negotiate deals for what they wear and promote when not playing – such as aftershaves or perfumes.
- **Transport and travel** – this can range from having a free car to being flown to different events by particular airlines. Even at lower levels, coach operators may arrange sponsorship deals.
- **Training** – assistance with training is provided, sometimes by subsidising time off work to train (for many amateur performers) or providing the equipment or facilities to allow the training to take place. Coaches and trainers can be provided and paid for by the sponsors.
- **Entry fees and expenses** – these can mount up and accommodation in particular can be very expensive if a lot of travel is involved. Many performers have negotiated deals with particular hotel chains.
- **Food** – sometimes a particular type of food is important, which can also provide a sponsorship opportunity.

Not all of these levels of sponsorships are available to all performers. Once again, the type is linked to the profile of the performer. A very successful elite performer is likely to get more sponsorship opportunities than a low-level beginner.

Benefits to the sponsors

- **Advertising** – this is the main benefit for sponsors. They have large advertising budgets and, since a great deal of sport is covered by the media, especially television, sponsorship is a good way of getting a company's product seen by millions of people. The advertising serves to increase sales and therefore profits for the company.
- **Image** – sport has a healthy, successful, positive image and it is a benefit for a company to be able to associate itself and its products with this image. The company also gains goodwill from helping out the sport, which helps to improve its image.
- **Tax relief** – companies are allowed to claim back a certain amount of the money they provide for sponsorship against the taxes they have to pay.
- **Research and development** – new products are tried out by the top-level performers to see how well they work.

> **Exam tip**
>
> The examiner is likely to ask a question regarding the ease of obtaining sponsorship at different levels. This may also be linked to what type of sponsorship this is most likely to be.

Advantages and disadvantages of sponsorship to sport

Advantages

- A lucrative sponsorship deal can allow the performer to concentrate on their sport. They can focus on training and then performing, without any financial worries.
- Specific sports can be promoted and developed, and become more successful.
- Competitions can be bigger and better, often with much higher levels of prize money being available.
- Both the profile and image of a sport can be raised and improved.

Disadvantages

- Dates can be changed to suit demands from sponsors. The start time of major events, in particular, will be arranged to coincide with peak-time television viewing. This can affect international sport, with the associated problems of time-zone differences around the world.
- Clothing/equipment restrictions – the type of clothing worn, or equipment used, may not always be the most suitable for the performer but they have to use it nonetheless.
- Withdrawal of sponsorship – sponsors are very sensitive about image and sponsorship deals can be withdrawn from performers if they are associated with anything bad. Having to maintain a 'squeaky clean' public image can add to the pressure on high-profile performers, and sudden collapses in sponsorship deals can make it difficult to maintain performance standards.
- Inequality – minority sports can find it very difficult to obtain any levels of sponsorship. This is also the case for performers within a minority sport, particularly low-level performers.

Exam tip

Make sure you know examples of the main advantages and disadvantages of sponsorship.

Typical mistake

Confusing the advantages and disadvantages of sponsorship between the *sponsors* and those being *sponsored* – they are very different!

Revision activity

Research the most recent high-profile sponsorship deal which an individual has been able to negotiate.

Now test yourself

TESTED

1 Which one of the following would not be a type of sponsorship an individual would receive?
   a) equipment
   b) bonuses
   c) accessories
   d) clothing. (1 mark)
2 Explain **two** benefits of sponsorship sponsors can gain. (4 marks)
3 Describe **two** advantages of sponsorship which sport can gain. (4 marks)

The media

The media includes all forms of mass communication. The media makes a very important contribution to sport in helping to give an understanding of performance and participation. The role of the various forms of the media in sport is considered below.

Television

There are different types of both coverage and ways in which TV is broadcast:

- **Coverage** – this includes live sporting programmes, highlights programmes, documentaries, quiz programmes, news bulletins, dedicated club channels (for major sports such as football), specific schools' programmes, skill development and instructional series, coaching series, magazine programmes, text information, interactive services offering alternative commentaries, views, action and information or events and competitions.
- **Types** – there are three main types of broadcast:
  - **Digital terrestrial television** – these are the main TV providers whose broadcasts can be accessed via a TV set with an aerial. In the UK these are BBC, ITV, Channel 4 and Channel 5.
  - **Satellite and digital broadcasters** – in the UK the main broadcaster is Sky Television (with a whole set of dedicated sports channels) but there are also BT Sport, Virgin Media, ESPN and Eurosport. The satellite broadcast also offers many other features such as 'catch-up', 'any time' and interactive options within each channel choice.
  - **Internet access** – both terrestrial and satellite providers offer access to their programmes via the internet. This means viewers can watch sports coverage on smart TVs, computers, laptops, tablets and mobile phones.

A crowd of press photographers covering a football match between Argentina and Germany.

Radio

Developments in radio broadcasting have led to an increase in the number of sports broadcasts. There are terrestrial broadcasters who broadcast on the traditional networks. There are also digital radio broadcasts which can be accessed through computers, satellite TV, mobile devices and DAB radios.

Radio broadcasters are able to provide most of the same services as TV providers can (except for actual pictures); however, they have the advantage of cheaper broadcasting costs (so companies can afford to cover more sports and fixtures). They also have the benefit of very wide access, as people can even listen to radios in their cars and (thanks to radio on mobile phones) virtually anywhere.

The press

This includes the following:

- **Newspapers** – these are printed and available daily (usually morning editions but also evening editions) and sport is always a major feature. It is traditional for sport to be featured at the back of each edition and there are usually sports 'supplements' on Saturdays and Sundays. The major newspapers now make their daily editions available digitally to be accessed on mobile devices, laptops and computers.
- **Magazines** – general magazines often have specific sports sections but there are also magazines linked to specific sports or activities, or to targeted readerships such as young males or females.
- **Books** – these can vary from educational textbooks (such as this one!) to coaching or instructional books, sporting autobiographies, rulebooks and sport-specific books. These are available either in hard copy or digitally via e-readers.

The internet

All of the forms of the media mentioned above can be accessed via the internet but it has other particular additional functions:

- **Search engines** – these allow information to be accessed, such as general information like facts and figures, and can also be used to search for sports-related websites.
- **Websites** – every sport and physical activity will have many websites, and sports associations and governing bodies have websites. Websites can provide an enormous range of information, opinion and discussion about every aspect of performance and participation in sport.
- **Social media** – using Facebook or Twitter allows up-to-date information and views to be shared, both about sport as a spectator and about ways to participate in sport and physical activity.

> **Exam tip**
>
> The examiner is likely to ask questions regarding the types of media which exist, linked to the types of output they are responsible for.

Media influences

The media is very influential in shaping views and opinions about performance and participation.

Exam tip

Make sure you know about media influences on performance and participation, both positive and negative. It would be useful to be able to give an example of both a positive and a negative influence.

Positive influences

- **Information provision and updating** – the media allows everyone to be kept up to date and informed. Both instruction and entertainment can be included. This can increase both support and participation by keeping individuals informed about what and where sport is occurring.
- **Educational uses** – TV companies provide school-level programmes on sport, coaching and skill development. This allows greater access for all learners.
- **Variety of content** – the media is able to provide a huge range of provision and output.
- **Demonstrating performance** – the visual aspect of TV, in particular, enables high standards of performance to be visible, while the use of technology such as slow-motion and action replays allows these to be analysed in detail. TVs (and computers) allow CDs, DVDs and hard-drive recordings to be used and replayed.
- **Revenue source** – TV providers, and satellite TV in particular, pay large amounts of money to be able to provide coverage of major sporting events. Stations often bid against each other and negotiate with the organisers (or specific clubs or sports) to decide the amounts they are willing to pay for exclusive coverage. TV companies even pay for the privilege of being able to broadcast highlights programmes, and the money they pay goes directly to the sports involved.
- **Links to sponsors** – companies sponsor sport in order to get more media attention for their products and services. The greater the media attention, the more sponsors will pay for it, which brings more money into the sport concerned.
- **Technological advances** – TV stations have developed new techniques to aid their sports coverage, especially in regard to checking officials' decisions, for example, tracking ball flights and impact points. These technological advances have often then been adopted by the sports to help officials make correct decisions and allow participants the option of reviewing decisions made by the officials.

Negative influences

- **Media pressure** – if the media decides to mount campaigns against a performer or team then this can be damaging for performance. For example, media pressure has led to managers and coaches being forced to resign their posts.
- **TV directors' influence** – directors of a TV broadcast can decide what events or sports are seen or highlighted. They can even decide what is to be said about the event or sport in terms of comments as commentary or summary discussions. This also applies in the written media, where opinions can be stated and justified.
- **Popularity** – if a sport is given a high media profile (this usually applies to TV) then it is likely to become more popular. This has been the case with both darts and snooker in recent years. Conversely, if a sport is not featured it is less likely to have high levels of participation and support.

- **Levels of support** – spectators may decide that it is an easier and cheaper option to watch an event on TV rather than attend in person. The supporters are still supporting, but now the club or organisation does not get the revenue from ticket sales, which can have a negative impact on their finances.
- **Undermining officials** – big screens and replays at sports grounds can show an incorrect decision, bad tackle, off-the-ball incident or foul play which the officials missed, and can even cause crowd unrest and poor behaviour.
- **Altered event timings** – many organisers are so closely linked to the media supporting their event that they are willing to change the start times and even dates to accommodate them. For example, the National Football League for American football requires twenty 'television time-outs' per game in order for TV commercials to be shown.
- **Intrusion** – at any event there may be a great many photographers, reporters, cameramen, sound technicians, cables, gantries and scaffolding, all of which can get in the way of the paying spectators or even distract the players.

Now test yourself

TESTED

1 Which one of the following would not be a form of the media?
   a) television
   b) the internet
   c) radio
   d) mobile phones. (1 mark)
2 Which one of the following would not be a form of the press?
   a) newspapers
   b) books
   c) social media
   d) magazines. (1 mark)
3 Describe **two** advantages which radio has over television as a form of the media. (4 marks)

Typical mistake

Thinking that the media only has positive influences, it can have some very negative influences as well!

Revision activity

Research an activity which has seen a rise in its profile due to media influences recently and one which has seen a decline in its profile over the same time-frame.

Positive and negative impacts of technology

There are three main areas in which technological developments have had an effect on participation and performance in different activities and for different performers.

Equipment

Developments in technology mean that new artificial materials have often replaced natural materials for making equipment. This generally makes the equipment lighter, stronger or more flexible, according to the specific needs of an activity:

- **Racket sports** – all rackets for tennis, badminton and squash were originally made of wood but they are now made of carbon-fibre, fibreglass, metal alloys such as titanium, and even ceramics. The strings are now nylon or polymer based, allowing for much greater tension to be added than could be used before. As the new materials are lighter, it also means that the racket head sizes can be increased without making the rackets any heavier.
- **Pole-vault** – in this event the pole itself has changed dramatically. It was originally made from bamboo or aluminium but now carbon-fibre and fibreglass are used to allow much greater heights to be reached. Because of this, the technology related to the landing areas also needed to be updated. Landing areas are now constructed of partially inflated high-tech foam between 1.0 and 1.5 metres thick. This allows the jumpers to land safely from heights in excess of 6 metres.
- **Safety equipment** – many sports, ranging from football to cricket, now make use of lighter, stronger materials which offer greater comfort and improved protection.

Materials

In general, these are the materials which are used for clothing and footwear:

- **Body suits** – first worn by swimmers in the 2000 Olympic Games to allow them to be more streamlined and achieve faster times. They proved so successful that they ended up being banned in 2010 because it was felt that some swimmers were gaining an unfair advantage. However, similar versions are still worn by some sprinters and cyclists to reduce the amount of drag or wind resistance.
- **Lighter clothing** – allows perspiration to disperse easily but still keeps the performer comfortable. This is particularly useful for a marathon runner. At the other extreme, waterproof clothing (for golfers in particular) and better-insulated clothing to retain heat have assisted in many outdoor and adventurous activities.
- **Footwear** – this is now very specific for every individual sport, with combinations of natural and synthetic materials making up different part of the shoes or boots. These are generally light, hard-wearing, strong and flexible, and offer more grip. They are also fully adjustable in terms of lacing-up and can even be partially inflatable to allow a perfect fit.

Facilities

Older, general sports facilities, such as halls and gyms catering for a variety of activities, are not always able to offer the specialised provision which many sports now need. Therefore these now tend to be purpose built:

- Stadiums are now purpose built and can include designs for athletics, rugby and football. Many existing stadiums are being updated and upgraded, with some clubs opting to sell the ones they own in order to move to build new and improved ones. Adding retractable roofs (such as the Millennium Stadium in Cardiff and the tennis courts at Wimbledon) has been made possible due to improved technology.
- Sports such as gymnastics have benefited from specialised facilities. These have allowed better and safer areas to both train and compete. For example, sprung floors (to enable tumbling) and safety pits beneath the specialist equipment enable the gymnasts to train more effectively.
- Training equipment available in specialised gyms means that training can now be very focused and specific. This helps to present opportunities for all and not just elite athletes.

Recording and analysing performance

There are a great many devices now available that allow performers to record, play back and analyse performances:

- **Video cameras** – these include standard cameras that also have a video function.
- **Flip-cams** – these often have built-in hard drives to store imagery but use memory cards as well. Replays can be shown on the device itself but can also be played through a laptop or computer.
- **Mobile phones** – camera and video camera functions on mobiles have now developed to the point where they are of similar quality to cameras and camcorders. These phones have the added benefit of being able to email or message images to other devices very quickly and easily.
- **Laptops** – these now have integrated cameras and also offer the facility to record and play back action.
- **Tablets** – these have the additional function of apps which can be bought and which can enhance the camera and video functions already on the devices. A commonly used app available on Apple's iPhones and iPads is known as Coach's Eye.

At the highest levels of sport there are additional devices used, especially for the accurate analysis of achievement:

- Electronic timing is used wherever possible and always at top-flight swimming and athletic events. To the human eye it can be difficult to judge positions that are very close, so very accurate timing, to one thousandth of a second, is used. In competitive swimming, swimmers touch sensor pads as they finish the race. In athletics, the timing devices are also linked to visual imagery and sensors.
- Tennis uses a device known as Cyclops to decide if serves land in or out. The machine is specifically calibrated to detect balls which have landed beyond the service line.

Exam tip

Make sure you know how technological innovations have led to improvements in sports performance and participation. It is a good idea to know some specific examples to use in your answers.

- Hawk-Eye is a ball-tracking technology used in tennis and cricket, and from August 2013 it was introduced for goal-line technology in football:
  - In tennis, this technology is able to accurately track the flight of a ball to tell if a tennis shot is in, on the line or out.
  - In cricket, it is used to see the flight a cricket ball would have continued on for leg-before-wicket decisions.
  - In football, it can judge if a shot crosses the line at football for a goal to be given.

  The officials are now able to make use of this technology to ensure that the decisions they make are correct. In both tennis and cricket, the players are given opportunities to challenge (in tennis) or review (in cricket) the decisions made.
- Many sports now have video officials (or extra officials) who are able to check replays of action, use the technology available and communicate with the officials in charge to either uphold or change decisions.

The technology used to record and analyse any performance is advancing at such a rate that even the recent examples given above are likely to be superseded or replaced quite quickly.

> **Exam tip**
>
> The examiner is likely to ask questions about the specific forms of technology which can be used to improve either knowledge or performance.

Goal-line technology was introduced into the Premiership in 2014 and is now used in all games. This photo shows the equipment being tested at Hull City's ground.

Improving knowledge and performance

Use of the internet, interactive tools and devices (and even in some cases games consoles) means that teaching and training aids are now available in abundance. Websites offer a wealth of information and computer programs are constantly being developed.

Data collection and analysis is relatively easily managed. For example, Prozone is a system used by the majority of football clubs. It provides extremely detailed performance–analysis software tracking the movements of every player on the pitch every tenth of a second and providing information on over 2500 actions in every match. To do this it makes use of 360° camera placement, using a minimum of eight digital cameras at all four corners of the stadium.

Typical mistake

Thinking that all technological advances have been allowed to be used. The body suits used by swimmers were subsequently banned and long-handled putters used by golfers were also eventually banned.

Revision activity

Keep an on-going record of advances in technology that sports have developed and now use which were not in existence when this book was published!

Now test yourself

1 All of the following are technological developments except:
   a) fibreglass for pole-vault poles
   b) ceramics for rackets
   c) polymers for racket strings
   d) sports vitamin supplements. (1 mark)
2 Body suits might be worn by cyclists to:
   a) match the designs and colours on their bikes
   b) keep them drier in wet conditions
   c) reduce wind resistance
   d) enable more space for advertising logos. (1 mark)
3 Choose one technological development and explain how it has helped to improve performance. (4 marks)
4 Hawk-Eye is currently being used in all of the following sports except:
   a) badminton
   b) football
   c) tennis
   d) cricket. (1 mark)
5 All of the following devices can be used for recording and analysing performance except:
   a) video cameras
   b) tape recorders
   c) laptops
   d) tablets. (1 mark)
6 Explain why some sports allow the use of technology such as Hawk-Eye. (4 marks)

5c Ethical issues

5.5 Conduct of performers

Conduct of performers

Performers in all levels of sport are expected to conduct themselves properly in the following areas of behaviour:

- **Etiquette** – this is not enforceable but it is an accepted way of behaving in certain situations. In football matches the referee has to stop the play to allow treatment for a player with a head injury. However, if players think an opponent is injured and requires immediate treatment they will kick the ball out of play to stop the action to allow a physio to give treatment. From the resulting throw-in, the opponents then throw the ball back to the team who initially kicked the ball out – an example of good etiquette from both teams.
- **Sportsmanship** – this is where performers conform to the rules and do not try to 'bend' them. Congratulating an opponent on a good shot in cricket, shaking their hand on completion of a century or being totally honest when they know a catch has not 'carried' are all examples of good sportsmanship.
- **Gamesmanship** – this is the exact opposite to sportsmanship as the rules are not actually broken but they are pushed to the limit. One of the most common examples of this is time wasting, especially in football, where a team can try to protect their lead by delaying play as much as they can until the 90 minutes are up.
- **Contract to compete** – all performers should be expected to conform to this as it encompasses all of the expected codes of conduct for a performer.

Prohibited substances

Prohibited substances are **drugs** that are banned for use by sports performers. They are also often referred to as performance-enhancing drugs.

Stimulants

Stimulants are substances that increase alertness, reduce **fatigue** and may increase competitiveness and hostility. They can also produce a loss of judgement and this can lead to accidents in some sports.

An overdose of stimulants can cause death. This has occurred twice in cycling events, once in an Olympic event and once in the Tour de France. Other side effects can include:

- high blood pressure and headaches
- strokes and increased and irregular heartbeats
- anxiety and tremors
- insensitivity to serious injuries
- addiction.

Etiquette A convention or unwritten rule in an activity. It is not an enforceable rule but it is usually observed

Sportsmanship Conforming to the rules, spirit and etiquette of a sport

Gamesmanship Attempting to gain an advantage by stretching the rules to the limit

Contract to compete Unwritten agreement to follow and abide by the written and unwritten rules

Drug A chemical substance which, when introduced to the body, can alter the biochemical system

Stimulants Drugs that have an effect on the central nervous system; they increase mental and/or physical alertness

Fatigue Either physical or mental; fatigue is a feeling of extreme or severe tiredness due to a build-up of lactic acid or working for long periods of time

Adrenaline A natural hormone released to speed the heart rate up

Narcotic analgesics

Narcotic analgesics include morphine, heroin and codeine. The main reasons they are banned is because they hide the effects of illness and injury. They suppress the feeling of pain but their side effects are:

- respiratory depression
- physical and psychological dependence
- exhaustion or overtraining
- constipation
- extreme apathy.

Performers must be very careful to draw the line between treating an injury and actually concealing its full extent by taking narcotic analgesics. A far more serious injury could occur and an addiction to these drugs can lead to death.

Anabolic agents

These are probably the best known and most commonly abused drugs in sport. The main type is known as androgenic **anabolic steroids**. These are a group of both natural and synthetic compounds which are very similar to testosterone, the natural male hormone. Testosterone has two main effects:

- **androgenic** – promotes the development of male characteristics
- **anabolic** – stimulates the build-up of muscle tissue.

There are well in excess of a hundred types of anabolic steroids available. The most common ones are nandrolone, testosterone, stanozolol and boldenone. These are taken in tablet form, but some of the steroids are taken by injection directly into the muscles.

Performers are tempted to use steroids as they feel it can help their performance by:

- increasing muscle strength
- enabling them to train harder and for longer
- increasing their competitiveness.

The risks and side effects of taking steroids are quite serious and include:

- Liver damage and heart disease.
- Sexual and physique problems – men can suffer from reduced sperm production and sterility. There can be shrinking and hardening of the testicles, impotence and even the growth of breasts. Women can have a disruption of the menstrual cycle and ovulation, changes in the sex organs, balding, acne, growth of facial hair and deepening of the voice.
- Behavioural effects – there can be quite marked changes of behaviour in some individuals. This can be seen as increased moodiness and aggression. The changes can be so extreme that they would constitute a psychiatric disorder.

Peptide hormones

Peptide hormones exist in the body normally but drug use increases the levels artificially and it is these higher levels which are tested for and banned. They include:

- **Erythropoietin (EPO)** – this naturally occurs in the kidneys and regulates production of red blood cells. It can have a similar effect to blood doping.
- Human growth hormone (HGH, somatrophin) – this is used to increase growth and can have some serious side effects including damaging the nervous system.

Narcotic analgesics Drugs that can be used to reduce the feeling of pain

Anabolic steroids Artificially produced male hormones mimicking testosterone. They promote muscle and bone growth, and reduce recovery time. Often used by power athletes such as sprinters

Peptide hormones Drugs that stimulate the production of naturally occurring hormones (such as EPO) which increase red blood cell count or oxygen-carrying capacity

Erythropoietin (EPO) A type of peptide hormone that increases the red blood cell count

---

Quick quizzes at www.hoddereducation.co.uk/myrevisionnotes

Diuretics

Diuretic drugs are used medically to reduce excess body fluids and for the management of high blood pressure. In sport they have been used to:

- Reduce weight quickly where weight categories are important, or being light is an advantage, such as with horseracing jockeys.
- Reduce the concentration of substances by diluting the urine. This effect leads to diuretics also often being referred to as 'masking agents', as they can reduce the concentration of other prohibited substances in the urine which may have to be produced for a drug test.

Prohibited methods (blood doping)

Blood doping is linked to prohibited substances, but is a method rather than a drug that is taken. It is a technique used by endurance athletes to make their blood more efficient in carrying and transporting oxygen. It involves a performer having a transfusion of blood (this is when blood is actually added back into the bloodstream). It can involve the performer having blood taken away, training with depleted blood levels, then having the blood replaced. It can even be replaced with someone else's blood, red blood cells or related products.

There was a time when this method was tolerated but it is now banned. Possible side effects include:

- development of allergic reactions such as a rash or fever
- acute kidney damage if the incorrect blood group is used
- delayed transfusion reaction which can result in a fever and jaundice
- transmission of infectious diseases such as viruses, including hepatitis and HIV
- overload of the circulation and metabolic shock.

Even though performance-enhancing drugs are banned and prohibited, and being caught can result in disqualification and lengthy bans, performers are tempted to take these drugs for the following reasons:

- increased chances of success
- the chance of increased fame
- the opportunity to increase wealth through prize money and sponsorship.

> **Diuretic drugs** Drugs that remove fluid from the body by increasing urine excretion
>
> **Blood doping** Defined by the World Anti-Doping Agency (WADA) as the misuse of techniques and/or substances to increase one's red blood cell count

Professional cyclist Lance Armstrong was banned from the sport for life. All his results from August 1998 were cancelled as a result of his long-term doping.

5c Ethical issues

AQA GCSE (9–1) PE   61

The disadvantages include:
- it is effectively cheating and immoral
- there are sometimes quite extreme associated health risks
- large fines are often levied if caught
- lengthy bans can be imposed – even lifetime ones
- the reputation of the performer is damaged – this can result in sponsors withdrawing and adverse publicity.

It is not only the performers who can lose out when they are caught taking prohibited drugs; the actual sport or event can have its reputation damaged and lose credibility.

Beta-blockers

Beta-blockers are a restricted class of drug, that is, a drug which can be prescribed by a medical professional for certain conditions, but the advantages gained by using them can be a benefit in some sporting activities.

Beta-blockers are taken to:
- reduce heart rate, muscle tension and blood pressure
- reduce the effects of adrenaline
- improve fine control and precision.

The side effects can include:
- nausea
- weakness
- heart problems.

Now test yourself

TESTED

1 All of the following are performance-enhancing drugs except:
   a) stimulants
   b) paracetamol
   c) diuretics
   d) peptide hormones. (1 mark)
2 All of the following are possible side effects of taking beta-blockers except:
   a) nausea
   b) weakness
   c) heart problems
   d) reduced heart rate. (1 mark)
3 What is meant by the term 'etiquette'? Give an example of a sportsperson displaying good etiquette. (4 marks)
4 Describe the difference between a performance-enhancing drug and a restricted class of drugs. (4 marks)

Revision activity

Research examples where the drugs described here have been used by a performer to gain an advantage in a specific sporting activity. Make a note of the particular performance-enhancing benefit that the performer was trying to achieve.

Beta-blockers Drugs that are used to steady nerves by controlling the heart rate. They have a calming and relaxing effect

Exam tip

Questions relating to performance-enhancing drugs will often focus on the particular advantages that each drug has for a performer in a particular sport. Subsidiary parts of the question are likely to focus on the disadvantages in terms of the side effects that can be experienced.

Typical mistake

Thinking that taking anabolic steroids automatically gives you bigger muscles! It is a training drug that increases the capacity to overload when training, which can then result in quicker and greater muscle gain.

5.6 Spectator behaviour

Spectator behaviour

Most major sporting events, matches and activities encourage spectators to attend. For many professional sports this is one of their main sources of income.

Spectators can have a positive influence in the following ways:
- the creation of an atmosphere
- it can provide a **home-field advantage** both for the home team and for individuals.

The negative influences of spectators include:
- Increased pressure from the home crowd can have a negative effect, especially if the home fans do not think their team is performing particularly well.
- There is often a potential for crowd trouble and possible hooliganism.
- A large crowd can lead to safety concerns and increased safety costs as the home team or club has a responsibility to its spectators. One of the biggest costs in football is that of providing stewards throughout the stands and pitch side, to keep rival sets of fans apart and also to prevent any pitch invasions.
- It could possibly have a negative effect on participation numbers among younger performers.

Hooliganism

There are various reasons why **hooliganism** occurs:
- **Rivalries** – often between sets of fans; this is very common where teams are geographically quite close together.
- **Hype** – the media can often agitate the situation by emphasising negative views and opinions and referring back to previous problems which may have existed.
- The situation can be heightened and fuelled by the fans taking drugs or consuming too much alcohol. This is one of the main reasons why alcohol is banned from football grounds and stadiums.
- **Associated gang culture** – some of these gangs decide to adopt and/ or associate themselves with particular teams or clubs. This is usually regional or city based as the gangs link themselves to local teams and clubs.
- **Frustration** – some fans can become very frustrated if their team is not doing well or if they feel that many of the official's decisions are going against them, and this can manifest itself in disorderly behaviour.
- **Displays of masculinity** – this is a particularly male characteristic often displayed by young males.

The rise of hooliganism and poor spectator behaviour at football matches in recent years has led to a number of measures and strategies being put in place to try to combat the problem:
- **Early kick-offs** – the main reason for this is to make sure that matches kick off before local pubs are open and to reduce the effect of excess alcohol consumption.
- **All-seater stadiums** – research has shown that spectators are more likely to behave if they are seated. This was also a measure introduced for pure safety reasons to ensure that there was no chance of overcrowding in areas of stadiums and arenas.

Home-field advantage Gaining an advantage in a sporting event from being in familiar surroundings with the majority of the spectators supporting you

Hooliganism Disorderly, aggressive and often violent behaviour by spectators at sporting events

Masculinity Displaying masculine (male) stereotypical behaviour

Revision activity

Research some examples where hooliganism has marred a sporting event and make a note of any security measures which were in place and the action which was taken to prevent this happening again.

- **Segregation of fans** – this takes part within the stadiums but the fans are also often escorted to and from the grounds by police and stewards to minimise the chances of clashes.
- **Improved security** – this includes a high police presence, a large number of trained and experienced stewards, and the use of CCTV cameras to monitor crowds and their behaviour.
- **Travel restrictions** – some fans can only travel with authorised companies, and the timing of their arrival and departure from the grounds is also controlled.
- **Banning orders** – those found guilty of inappropriate behaviour and hooliganism can be criminally prosecuted and banned by clubs from attending any fixtures.
- **Educating fans** regarding appropriate behaviour expected and demanded has helped, and many campaigns and promotional activities have been launched to help to improve the situation.

There is a very fine balance between making sure that measures to combat hooliganism are effective and the very real problem of the high costs of providing security versus the safety of the spectators.

Trained and experienced stewards are employed by football clubs to ensure crowd safety and good behaviour at matches.

Now test yourself

1 All of the following are possible negative influences of spectator behaviour at matches or events except:
   a) safety costs
   b) possible crowd trouble
   c) creation of atmosphere
   d) reducing participation numbers among younger performers.
      (1 mark)
2 All of the following are positive influences spectators can have except:
   a) they can establish rivalries with opposing fans
   b) they create an atmosphere
   c) they provide home-field advantage
   d) they can provide revenue. (1 mark)
3 Identify and explain two reasons why hooliganism occurs. (4 marks)
4 Describe the possible negative effects a large crowd of spectators can have. (4 marks)

Summary

This chapter concentrates on developing your knowledge and understanding of the socio-cultural factors that impact on physical activity and sport, and the impact on society.

The main areas for you to review, revise and be aware of are as follows:
- The engagement patterns of different social groups and the factors affecting participation.
- The role and influence of commercialisation of physical activity and sport.
- The types of sponsorship which are available and the links between sponsorship and the media.
- The positive and negative impacts of sponsorship and the media on performers, sport, officials, the audience or spectators, and the sponsor or company.
- The positive and negative impacts of technology on performers, sport, officials, the audience or spectators, and the sponsor or company.
- The different types of technology currently used in sport.
- Ethical and socio-cultural issues in physical activity and sport.
- The conduct of performers.
- The different categories of prohibited substances and the basic positive and negative side-effects of these.
- Prohibited methods (blood doping) and the effects and side effects of using these methods.
- Drugs which are subject to certain restrictions – such as beta-blockers.
- Which type of performers may use different types of performance-enhancing drugs, with a knowledge of examples of this occurring.
- The disadvantages to the sport or event of performers taking performance-enhancing drugs.
- Spectator behaviour – notably the positive and negative effects of spectators at matches and events.
- The reasons why hooliganism occurs.
- The strategies which are employed to combat hooliganism and poor spectator behaviour.

6 Health and fitness

6.1 Physical, emotional and social health, fitness and well-being

REVISED

You need to be able to link levels of participation in physical activity, exercise and sport to **health**, well-being and **fitness**. You need to be aware too of how exercise can suit and also benefit the varying needs of different people. You will also find that many of the headings and topics link very closely to other areas of this book and other topics already covered.

Physical health and well-being

Benefits include:
- improving the heart function (see Section 1.3, page 6)
- improving the efficiency of the body systems (see Sections 1.1–1.3, pages 1–6)
- reducing the risks of some illnesses
- increasing the ability to do everyday tasks – this is linked very closely to the components of fitness (see Section 3.1, pages 20–1) as good flexibility, endurance and strength are essential for many everyday tasks
- helping to avoid **obesity**.

Mental health and well-being

Taking some regular physical exercise can help to improve your mental health and general well-being, as the benefits identified below indicate. Taking exercise can result in a feeling of being 'pleasantly tired', and this in turn helps to regulate more regular and restful sleep patterns.

Participating in physical activity can have the following benefits on mental health and well-being:
- a reduction in the levels of stress and tension (see Section 4.3, page 39)
- the release of feel-good hormones such as **serotonin**
- helps with the ability to control emotions.

Social health and well-being

Regularly participating in physical activity, exercise and sport also offers the opportunity for participants to improve their social well-being and therefore gain the following benefits:
- increased opportunities to socialise and make friends
- increased opportunities to be actively involved in cooperation with other people
- increased opportunities to be involved in teamwork
- helps to ensure that you have the essential human needs of food, shelter and clothing.

> **Health** A state of complete physical, mental and social well-being, and not merely the absence of disease or infirmity
>
> **Fitness** The ability to meet or cope with the demands of the environment
>
> **Obesity** Being obese is to be overweight, caused by an imbalance of calories consumed to energy expended
>
> **Serotonin** A chemical found in the human body that is responsible for maintaining mood balance – a deficit of serotonin can lead to depression

> **Exam tip**
>
> Remember that questions on this topic relate to exercise at a fairly basic level and would not be related to an elite performer level.

Fitness

Fitness is one aspect of health, fitness and well-being. There are different types of fitness:

- **general fitness** – the level of fitness suitable for a beginner standard performer
- **specific fitness** – the level of fitness required for an elite standard performer in the same activity.

Regular exercise maintains both health and fitness in the following ways:

- It helps to provide the levels of strength and stamina needed for everyday life. For example, jobs that involve repeated manual tasks such as stacking shelves, or jobs that require you to be on your feet all day.
- It maintains basic levels of flexibility to be able to cope with everyday living and without suffering discomfort. For example, being able to bend sufficiently to tie up shoelaces or reach up to get a book from a shelf.
- It reduces the chances of injury.
- It should enable the individual to maintain a good level of fitness.

Typical mistake

Fitness is not something which can be very quickly acquired. You need a good level of general fitness as a starting point before you can go on to gain specific fitness.

Many outdoor jobs ensure a healthy, active lifestyle.

Sedentary lifestyle

While people with jobs involving manual labour are already taking regular exercise as part of what they do, many people today have sedentary jobs. And while some people have outdoor jobs, most people work inside, away from fresh air and natural light. So for a lot of people their lifestyle involves making choices, for example:

- walking or cycling to work or school, instead of using a car or public transport
- taking part in some practical activity leisure pursuits like swimming or taking part in sports.

The consequences of a **sedentary lifestyle** can include:

- weight gain and even possible obesity
- increased rate of heart disease
- **hypertension**
- increased risk of contracting diabetes
- poor sleep patterns
- poor self-esteem
- increased **lethargy**.

Revision activity

Keep a diary or log for one month that records your 'lifestyle' in terms of how active you are and when you consider you have any sedentary phases.

Sedentary lifestyle A routine with irregular or no physical activity

Hypertension High blood pressure in the arteries

Lethargy A state of being drowsy, listless, unenergetic or even lazy

Now test yourself

TESTED

1 Which of the following would *not* be considered to be a sedentary job?
   a) office worker
   b) lorry driver
   c) telesales worker
   d) farmer. (1 mark)
2 Which of the following would *not* be a consequence of a sedentary lifestyle?
   a) hypertension
   b) poor sleep
   c) increased serotonin levels
   d) lethargy. (1 mark)
3 Define what is meant by good health. (3 marks)
4 Why is it important to be able to have flexibility for everyday living? (3 marks)

6.2 Somatotypes and obesity

Somatotype

Somatotype is a method of classifying body types first proposed by William Herbert Sheldon in the 1940s, when he identified three distinct, and extreme, body types. Very few people fit neatly or completely into one of these extremes but they are likely to favour one more than another in general terms. There are three identified body types or somatotypes:

- **Ectomorph** – typically has narrow shoulders and narrow hips. Ectomorphs tend to be tall and thin with a delicate build and are lightly muscled. They are therefore suited for endurance-type events.
- **Mesomorph** – typically has a muscular appearance with wide shoulders and narrow hips. Mesomorphs tend to have a muscular, athletic build with little body fat and are able to gain muscle relatively easily. They are therefore suited to specific sports requiring speed, strength and power.
- **Endomorph** – a pear-shaped body or fatness with wide hips and narrow shoulders. This type tends to have a rounded appearance, has trouble losing weight, but can gain muscle. Endomorphs are most suited to specific sports that do not require high levels of speed or mobility, due to their additional weight.

> **Somatotype** A method of classifying body type into the three categories of ectomorph, mesomorph and endomorph

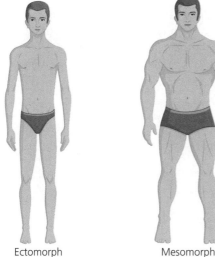

Ectomorph   Mesomorph   Endomorph

Figure 1 Extreme somatotypes.

These are the descriptions of extreme ectomorphs, mesomorphs and endomorphs – these extremes are not very common. Most individuals have a combination of the three types.

An individual's body type can make them more or less suited to a particular sporting activity or a particular playing position or role within a sport.

> **Exam tip**
>
> Make sure you know reasons why a particular body type might make a person particularly suited to a particular sport, playing position or role.

Obesity

Obesity is a term used to describe people who are overweight, caused by an imbalance of calories consumed to energy expended. A body mass index (BMI) of over 30 or being over twenty per cent above the standard weight-for-height ratio would be considered obese.

It is important not to confuse obesity with a body type (an error sometimes made in relation to an endomorph) as it is a condition, not a body type. However, being obese can affect performance in physical activity and sport in the following ways:

- Components of fitness:
  - it can limit stamina and cardio-vascular endurance
  - it limits flexibility
  - it limits agility
  - it limits speed and power.
- Physical factors:
  - possible increased chances of cancer
  - increased chances of heart disease and **heart attacks** (see Section 3.1, page 20)
  - increased chance of diabetes
  - increased chance of high cholesterol.
- Mental factors:
  - generally, causes **ill health**
  - increased chance of depression
  - loss of confidence.
- Social factors:
  - a possible inability to socialise
  - the possible inability to leave home – this is quite common in extreme cases.

Typical mistake

An endomorph is not necessarily obese and it is important not to confuse obesity with body type.

Revision activity

Match either a physical activity or sport where being obese would affect the level of performance for the four components of fitness listed above. List actual examples rather than just naming the activity or sport.

Heart attack This happens when the flow of oxygen-rich blood to a section of a heart muscle suddenly becomes blocked

Ill health A state of poor physical, mental and/or social well-being

---

Now test yourself

TESTED ☐

1 An endomorph has all of the following except:
   a) wide hips
   b) narrow shoulders
   c) pear-shaped body
   d) suitability to speed and mobility activities. (1 mark)
2 Which of these activities would an ectomorph be best suited to take part in?
   a) weightlifting
   b) swimming
   c) long-distance running
   d) high jump (1 mark).
3 Which of the following is not a somatotype?
   a) obesity
   b) mesomorph
   c) endomorph
   d) ectomorph. (1 mark)
4 Explain why suffering from obesity may affect performance in physical activity and sport in each of the following categories:
   a) physical factors
   b) mental factors
   c) social factors. (6 marks)

6.3 Diet, energy use, nutrition and hydration

Maintaining a balanced diet

It is essential to have a **balanced diet** so that the body is able to receive the nourishment required to maintain good physical health.

Everyone needs food to survive, and nutrients are the substances that make up food. The correct mixture of food and nutrients needs to be consumed. A balanced diet should contain 55–60 per cent carbohydrates, 25–30 per cent fat and 15–20 per cent protein. The reasons a balanced diet is needed include:

- unused energy is stored as fat, which could cause obesity (particularly saturated fat)
- suitable energy can be available for activity
- the body needs nutrients for energy, growth and **hydration**.

> **Balanced diet** Eating the right amount (for energy expended), the right amount of calories according to how much you are exercising, and different food types to provide nutrients, vitamins and minerals
>
> **Hydration** Having enough water to enable normal functioning of the body

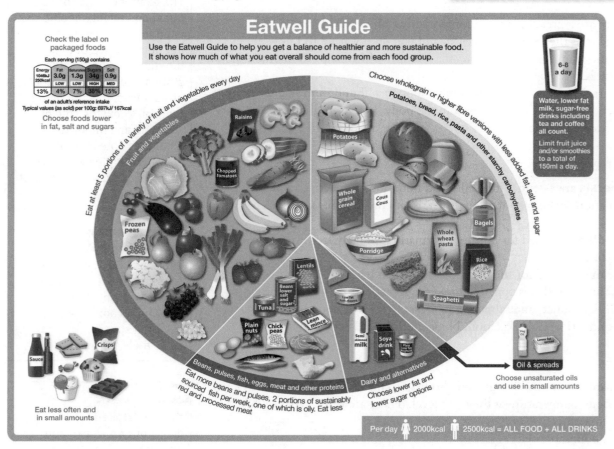

The nutrients that make up a balanced diet together with appropriate portion sizes.

Carbohydrates

Carbohydrates are the main energy source for the body. There are two categories of carbohydrates:

- **simple carbohydrates** found in foods such as sugar, milk and fruit
- **complex carbohydrates** found in foods such as bread, pasta, potatoes, rice and pulses or beans.

Carbohydrates are stored as glycogen in the liver and muscles. Glycogen can be used to provide energy during exercise.

Endurance athletes and performers often **carbo-load** (also known as carbohydrate loading) as a way of preparing themselves for a particular event or competition in order to increase their energy levels.

> **Carbo-load** Eating foods that are high in starch to increase carbohydrate reserves in muscles.

Proteins

These are often called 'building blocks' because they are needed in the growth of new tissue. They are very important for muscle growth and repair. Proteins are obtained from two sources:

- **animal protein** from fish, chicken and red meat
- **vegetable protein** from pulses (beans), grains and foods produced from animal products such as eggs, milk and cheese.

Some performers will select a **high protein diet**. These are usually bodybuilders or weightlifters aiming to build muscle and lose fat.

Vitamins

Vitamins are essential to enable you to maintain good health. Only small quantities are needed and these are usually contained in a normal healthy diet.

There are a great many different vitamins (all given a letter of the alphabet as they were discovered) and you do not need to know about specific vitamins. An example of a vitamin which helps to maintain good health is given below:

- **Vitamin A** – this is a fat-soluble substance found in milk and dairy products and it can be stored in the body. It helps to maintain healthy eyes, skin and bones.

Minerals

Minerals are essential for health and bone and connective tissue formation. Examples of these minerals and the benefits which they bring are:

- **iodine** – needed for hormone formation, notably from the thyroid gland
- **iron** – needed for the transport of oxygen by the red blood cells
- **calcium** – this is contained in dark green leafy vegetables, broccoli, milk products and salmon, and is essential for strong bones, muscle contraction and relaxation, blood clotting and nerve function.

Fats

Fats are a source of energy and also help to insulate the body and to keep the body temperature at the right level. There are three types of fats:

- saturated
- monounsaturated
- polyunsaturated.

Fats are found in many foods, including cheese, cream, meat, cooking oils, butter and margarine.

It is important to control the amount of fat in the diet because too much fat can be the main cause of gaining overall body weight.

High protein diet Eating foods that contain a lot of protein while reducing the intake of carbohydrates and fats. This has been linked to kidney problems

Minerals Inorganic substances which assist the body with many of its functions – such as bone formation (calcium)

Exam tip

The examiner will not ask questions about specific vitamins and minerals but being aware of their function, and being able to state some examples, could be required. It is important that you know the role of vitamins and minerals and being able to quote actual examples will make answering a question of that nature much easier.

Typical mistake

Vitamins and minerals are constituent parts of many foods eaten in a balanced diet and do not have to be taken specifically and separately.

Revision activity

Keep a detailed food diary for two weeks and accurately record your intake during that period. You will find very detailed information on the food packaging regarding what your foods consist of.

Water and fluids

The human body is mostly water (about 70 per cent). On average we lose about 2.5 litres of water from our body every day.

Water is a means of transport for nutrients, waste and hormones. Failure to replace water can result in **dehydration**, which can cause serious problems such as heat exhaustion. It is important to replace the water you lose, by drinking. If you fail to do so your body will weaken to the point where it will stop functioning.

The following will affect how quickly water is lost:
- the intensity of any work or exercise being carried out
- the amount of time spent exercising
- the temperature and humidity of your environment.

The main reason for maintaining water balance is to prevent dehydration as this results in the following:
- blood thickening (increased **viscosity**), which slows blood flow
- increases in heart rate as the heart has to work harder; this can result in an irregular heart rate or rhythm
- an increase in body temperature and overheating
- the slowing of reactions and increased reaction times, resulting in poorer decision making
- the onset of muscle fatigue or cramps.

Dehydration Excessive loss of body water interrupting the function of the body

Viscosity Thickening of the blood

Exam tip

You are likely to be asked questions relating to being able to understand and evaluate the consequences of dehydration to performance in different sporting activities.

Energy use

Energy is measured in **calories** and the energy you need is obtained from the food you eat. The amount of energy you require will be a factor to consider in terms of diet. You also need some energy just to keep your body working at rest. The average adult male requires 2500 kcal/day and the average adult female requires 2000 kcal/day. However, this varies depending on:

- age
- gender
- height
- energy expenditure (exercise).

> **Calorie** A unit which measures heat or energy production in the body (normally expressed as kcal)

Specific requirements for different performers

Dietary needs vary between people taking part in different physical activities. Performers need to be aware of this and vary their diet accordingly. Some examples are as follows:

- Female gymnasts need to be small and light and therefore should be careful to avoid too much fatty food.
- A weightlifter needs to be quite large and bulky, so additional fats and proteins may be needed.
- A soccer player has to make sure that they have enough energy-providing food for a 90-minute game.
- A marathon runner may have a high carbohydrate diet and specifically carbo-load for several days just before a race. They may even attend specially organised pasta parties to help them prepare.

What time you eat is also an important factor and the following need to be taken into account:

- **Before activity** – it is not wise to eat too close to taking part in physical activity and a performer should wait for two hours after eating.
- **During activity** – generally it is not recommended to eat during physical activity, although small quantities, for example fruit such as bananas, are all right.
- **After activity** – the same two-hour gap should be left after physical activity before eating substantial amounts. However, drinking liquids straight away is a good thing.

Planning a diet for a sports performer is usually a long-term exercise and is often carried out over a substantial period of time.

Now test yourself

TESTED

1 Which of the following is *not* a basic component of a healthy balanced diet?
   a) carbohydrates
   b) calories ✓
   c) fats
   d) proteins. (1 mark)
2 Explain what is meant by 'nutrition'. (3 marks)
3 For the following two specific diets, identify the type of sport each would be most appropriate for:
   a) plenty of carbohydrates, including attending a pasta party and carbo-loading just before an event
   b) avoiding too many fatty foods in order to keep body weight regulated, but ensuring that enough proteins and carbohydrates are included to maintain energy levels. (2 marks)
4 Why do the organisers of marathon races place water stations at regular intervals along the route? (2 marks)

Summary

This chapter concentrates on developing your knowledge and understanding of the benefits of participating in physical activity and sport to health, fitness and well-being.

The main areas for you to review, revise and be aware of are as follows:

- Being able to make the link between physical activity, exercise and sport to health, well-being and fitness, and how exercise can suit the varying needs of different people.
- How taking part in physical activity, exercise and sport can increase physical health and well-being.
- How taking part in physical activity, exercise and sport can increase mental health and well-being.
- How taking part in physical activity, exercise and sport can increase social health and well-being.
- How taking part in physical activity, exercise and sport can increase fitness.
- The consequences of a sedentary lifestyle and what is meant by sedentary.
- What is meant by obesity and how it might affect performance in physical activity and sport.
- What is meant by the term somatotype and the three extreme classifications of endomorph, ectomorph and mesomorph.
- Being able to identify, and justify, the most suitable body type (somatotype) for particular sports or positions within a sport.
- What is meant by energy use and how it is measured.
- The four factors of age, gender, height and energy expenditure in relation to energy use.
- Understanding what nutrition is and the reasons for having a balanced diet.
- The different types of food required to provided suitable nutrients, vitamins and minerals.
- The role of carbohydrates, fat, protein, vitamins and minerals.
- What is meant by hydration and the reasons for maintaining water balance.
- Being able to evaluate the consequences of dehydration to performance in different sporting activities.

Answers

Page 3

1 a) (1 mark)
2 b) (1 mark)
3 c) (1 mark)
4 Shoulder, elbow and wrist (3 marks).

Page 5

1 a) (1 mark)
2 d) (1 mark)
3 Any two major muscle groups (1 mark for each) from:
   - Deltoids
   - Trapezius
   - Latissimus dorsi
   - Pectorals
   - Biceps
   - Triceps
   - Abdominals (2 marks).

Page 9

1 a) (1 mark)
2 Up to 4 marks for four differences:
   - An artery has a thicker wall than a vein
   - The vein wall is thinner and less elastic
   - Veins have valves to make sure that the blood cannot flow backwards
   - Arteries carry oxygenated blood and veins carry deoxygenated blood (4 marks)
3 b) (1 mark)
4 Up to 4 marks for the following:
   - The diaphragm flattens and moves downwards
   - The intercostal muscles contract
   - This contraction causes the ribs to raise up
   - This makes the chest cavity larger
   - This has the effect of reducing air pressure inside the chest
   - This in turn causes air to be sucked into the lungs (4 marks).

Page 11

1 b) (1 mark)
2 1 mark for the definition and 3 marks for three clear explanatory points; for example:
   - It is a mild poison and a waste product of anaerobic exercise
   - It builds up in the muscles after exercise has finished
   - The most effective way of removing it is to complete a thorough cool-down once the exercise period has been completed (4 marks)
3 Up to 2 marks for each of the following:
   - Cool down – this allows the lactic acid to disperse safely and helps to maintain the elevated breathing rate and heart rate (and therefore the blood flow). Including some gentle stretching as part of this process is also beneficial
   - Manipulation of diet – this includes ensuring that you rehydrate and it is also advisable to take on carbohydrates as an additional energy source
   - Ice baths/massage – the main reason for performers using this method is to prevent DOMS (delayed onset muscle soreness). Massage, in particular, helps to increase blood flow to the sore area (6 marks).

Page 13

1 c) (1 mark)
2 Award up to 2 marks for the definition and a further 3 marks for correctly identifying a specific performer and identifying the benefits to be gained:
   - Increasing the size of the heart
   - An endurance event athlete/performer
   - This would make the heart more efficient
   - An increase in the oxygen-carrying capacity of the heart
   - This in turn would help to improve cardio-vascular endurance (5 marks)
3 Up to 2 marks for each of the following:
   - Increased tiredness/causing fatigue
   - A feeling of light headedness/possible nausea
   - Aching muscles/possible delayed onset muscle soreness (DOMS) (6 marks).

Page 16

1 a) (1 mark)
2 b) (1 mark)
3 Up to 3 marks for the following:
   - A rigid bar (bone)
   - Which turns about an axis
   - To create movement

- Each lever contains a fulcrum – the fixed point the lever is placed on/it requires effort to move this (3 marks)
4 Up to 3 marks for the following: the effort/divided by/the weight (also known as resistance) arm (3 marks).

Page 19

1 d) (1 mark)
2 a) (1 mark)
3 Up to 3 marks for the following:
- The elbow bends/flexes as the arms are raised
- The flexion is maintained as the arms are raised past the head and behind the shoulders
- As the elbows come past the head and shoulders the elbow straightens/flexes as it moves through
- The elbow joint is straight as the throw is completed (3 marks)
4 Up to 3 marks for the following:
- Sagittal plane (moving forwards)
- Transverse plane – rotating around the longitudinal axis
- Longitudinal axis (3 marks).

Page 21

1 b) (1 mark)
2 d) (1 mark)
3 a) (1 mark)
4 Award up to 4 marks for the following:
- The time taken to initiate a response/from a stimulus/in this case responding to the sound of the starting gun/which would enable the start to be as quick and efficient as possible/ensuring you are not then behind other sprinters in the race
- The initiation of a response/starting to lift and raise from the starting blocks/as the gun sound is heard/getting into a sprinting stride as quickly as possible/to gain the maximum advantage over the other runners (4 marks).

Page 24

1 c) (1 mark)
2 b) (1 mark)
3 Up to 6 marks for the following:
- It tests the component of flexibility/which is the range of movements possible at a joint/ in this case the hamstrings
- Makes use of a sit and reach box/with a slider or measuring tape or ruler you should sit on the floor with legs straight out and in front of you – not wearing shoes

- Set the measuring tape (slider) at 0 centimetres level with your feet and parallel with the legs
- Put the soles of your feet, shoulder width apart against the box
- Make sure the knees are held flat against the floor
- Reach gently towards your feet, with your hands on top of each other and palms facing down. Reach as far as possible, without bouncing
- After three practice reaches, the fourth is held for at least two seconds
- The distance your fingers reach is the score measured in centimetres (6 marks).

Page 26

1 b) (1 mark)
2 d) (1 mark)
3 Award up to 3 marks for each correctly selected and described principle.

Specificity within a training programme will vary according to the type of person who is training. It will depend on their initial fitness levels, body type and physiological factors, as well as other individual differences/the type of activity being trained for. It will depend on the sport itself and the level at which it is to be performed.

Specificity definition: making training specific to the sport being played/movements used/muscles used/energy system(s) used. A suitable practical example must also be given.

Progressive overload. You must build progressive overload into a training programme and always bear in mind the following points: the levels of general and specific fitness in place at the start of the programme. You may have to start very gradually but you must increase the demands as your body adjusts to the work it is doing and the stresses it is experiencing. Levels of plateauing occur where you progress to a certain level then seem to get stuck there before being able to move on – this can happen more than once.

Progression definition: gradually and safely increasing the amount of training that you do. Progressive overload is linked to the FITT acronym, which stands for:
- frequency, or how often training takes place; training more often increases overload
- intensity, of how hard you train; extra amounts of activity or increasing weights (if these are being used), increases overload
- the time, or duration, of each session; increasing the actual amount of time spent training, or even on one particular aspect of the training, also increases overload
- type.

Progressive overload is a gradual increase of the amount of overload so that fitness gains occur, but without potential for injury. Overload is the gradual increase of stress placed on the body during exercise training (more than usual). A suitable practical example must also be given.

Reversibility will be felt if, for any reason, training either stops or is reduced. Positive effects will be lost at roughly the rate of one-third of the time it took to gain them! A beginner loses effects at a faster rate than a regular, trained performer. Different factors of fitness may be affected in different ways and to different degrees.

Reversibility definition: losing fitness levels when you stop exercising. A suitable practical example must also be given.

Tedium will be experienced if all of the training becomes repetitive for each session as this is going to have negative effect and almost certainly prevent progress/progression.

Tedium definition: this is boredom that can occur from training the same way every time. Variety is needed. A suitable practical example must also be given (6 marks).

Page 28

1 d) (1 mark)
2 c) (1 mark)
3 Award up to 4 marks for the following:
 - To ensure that more time is given for the muscles or muscle groups to recover
 - To avoid tiring those muscles so they are not able to contract properly/to reduce the effects of fatigue setting in
 - To avoid any possibility of injury/or overuse problems (4 marks).

Page 30

1 220, minus age (15), which is 205 (3 marks)
2 b) (1 mark)
3 Award up to 4 marks for the following:
 - Repetitions are the number of times you perform a particular exercise/such as performing a one arm curl. Sets are the number of times you carry out an activity/the total arm curls performed would be one set (4 marks)
4 Award up to 3 marks for the following:
 - This can cause the muscles to be stretched beyond their normal range/this is then possibly dangerous/and can result in a muscle tear/ muscle strain (3 marks).

Page 33

1 b) (1 mark)
2 a) (1 mark)
3 Award up to 6 marks for the following:
 - Allowing the body to recover/from the intensive exercise preceding this phase
 - The removal of lactic acid/carbon dioxide/and waste products
 - Helps to prevent delayed onset muscle soreness/DOMS (6 marks).

Page 35

1 c) (1 mark)
2 b) (1 mark)
3 A named physical activity must be given and award up to 6 marks for the following:
 - A self-paced skill is one which is started when the performer decides to start it (the speed, rate or pace of the skill is controlled by the performer). An example of this is serving in tennis, as you would decide when and where to throw the ball up, when to make contact and where to aim it
 - An externally paced skill is one where the skill is started by an external factor (the speed, rate or pace of the skill is controlled by external factors such as an opponent) – so receiving the ball from a tennis serve would be started by your opponent serving to you (6 marks).

Page 37

1 a) (1 mark)
2 b) (1 mark)
3 Award up to 6 marks for the following:
 - Visual – as use could be made of demonstrations/videos and photographs to see/how moves should be performed most effectively
 - Verbal – from a coach/using technical terms/ which an elite performer would be aware of
 - Manual – actual physical assistance could be provided/such as helping them to perform a full rotation (6 marks).

Page 39

1 c) (1 mark)
2 a) (1 mark)
3 Award up to 6 marks for the following:
 - Over-arousal – being too aroused/in terms of alertness and readiness/can result in a low

point on the graph/as too much anxiety and pressure can be problematic for a performer
- Under-arousal – not being ready for the task in hand/possibly lethargic or not in an alert or ready enough state/results in being at a low point on the graph/probably resulting in under-achieving or not being interested or ready enough to perform (6 marks).

Page 41

1 a) (1 mark)

2 d) (1 mark)

3 Award up to 6 marks for the following by considering what intrinsic motivation is, and the reasons why it is more suitable:
- This is the drive from within, such as for pride/satisfaction/a sense of accomplishment or self-worth. A performer may get a real sense of personal achievement/self-satisfaction. Runners who are able to beat previous personal bests/or golfers who are able to reduce their handicaps/are two examples of performers attaining intrinsic motivation. Extrinsic factors such as awards medals, trophies and 'winning' are far more difficult to achieve and it can be 'demotivating' if they are failed or not achieved – which is highly likely for a beginner (6 marks).

Page 46

1 c) (1 mark)

2 Award up to 4 marks for the following:
- Boys tend to overtake girls in terms of height/weight and strength/they have greater muscle mass/these are all physiological factors which can give them an unfair advantage/for example height in basketball, weight and strength in rugby (4 marks)

3 Award up to 4 marks for the following:
- The culture might have dress codes, especially for women/which would make it difficult to compete or take part/religions (linked to cultures) may find some activities unsuitable or ban taking part at certain religious festivals/or have particular dietary restrictions/one particular sport may be very popular in one culture (such as cricket in India) so have particularly high levels of participation (4 marks)

4 c) (1 mark)

5 Award up to 4 marks for the following:
- Younger age children have a very a similar physiology/as they get older age becomes

more of a factor/also levels of competitive sport are greater/as older children are able to cope with more difficult tasks/in an attempt to make levels of size and strength more equal/and therefore less dangerous/age divisions are used to make it fairer and safer (4 marks)

6 Adapted activities/adapted equipment/disability classifications/provision for disabled people (4 marks).

Page 50

1 b) (1 mark)

2 Award up to 4 marks for the following:
- Advertising/the sport is covered by the media/so the company's product is seen by viewers/this serves to increase sales/therefore profits are also increased (4 marks)
- Image/the good image of the sport or individual is associated with the sponsor/the company gains goodwill from helping out the sport
- Tax relief/companies can claim back some of the money/against the taxes they have to pay
- Research and development/new products are tried out by top-level performers/to see how well they work (4 marks)

3 Award up to 4 marks for the following:
- Big lucrative sponsorship deals allow the performer to concentrate on their sport/they can focus on training/and then their performing
- Specific sports can be promoted/then they are developed/and then become more successful/popular
- Competitions can be bigger and better/often with higher levels of prize money available/therefore becoming more popular
- The image/and profile of the sport can be raised/and therefore improved (4 marks).

Page 54

1 d) (1 mark)

2 c) (1 mark)

3 Award up to 4 marks for the following:
- Radio is cheaper to broadcast/it needs less staff/employees to provide the coverage/radios are far more portable than televisions and receive more regular signals/radios can be listened to in cars/radios have wider access (4 marks).

Page 58

1 **d)** (1 mark)

2 **c)** (1 mark)

3 Award up to 4 marks for each correctly identified technological development and the correct explanation regarding how it has helped to improve performance. Example:
   - Improved materials for tennis rackets/these are now lighter and easier to grip/more power can be generated by the increased tension of the stings and stringing/the racket head size is also increased/allowing a greater contact area/the rackets are more durable and longer lasting/therefore less expensive in the long run (4 marks)

4 **a)** (1 mark)

5 **b)** (1 mark)

6 Award up to 4 marks for the following:
   - Any sport involving the need for ball tracking can make use of the technology/it can help officials make difficult decisions/helps to ensure correct decisions are made/allows players and performers to challenge decisions which they may think were incorrect/makes competition fairer/helps coaches to analyse performances in more detail and more accurately (4 marks).

Page 62

1 **b)** (1 mark)

2 **d)** (1 mark)

3 Award up to 4 marks for the following:
   - A convention/or unwritten rule in an activity. It is not an enforceable rule/but it is usually observed. An example would be kicking the football out of play/in order for an injured player to receive treatment/as the game is stopped/and physios are allowed on the pitch (4 marks)

4 Award up to 4 marks for the following:
   - A performance-enhancing drug is one whose use is banned/illegal (examples of these can be given, such as anabolic agents, diuretics and so on) and the performers choose to take them to improve their performance/as a form of cheating/restricted drugs can be prescribed by a medical professional/they would be required to help, manage or cure a medical condition/they would not be deemed to be cheating if they medically prescribed (4 marks).

Page 65

1 **c)** (1 mark)

2 **a)** (1 mark)

3 Award up to 4 marks for the following:
   - Rivalries – often between sets of fans, this is very common where teams are geographically quite close together
   - Hype – the media can often agitate the situation by emphasising negative views and opinions and referring back to previous problem which may have existed
   - The situation can be heightened and fuelled by the fans taking drugs or consuming too much alcohol. This is one of the main reasons why alcohol is banned from football grounds and stadiums
   - Associated gang culture – some of these gangs decide to adopt and/or associate themselves with particular teams or clubs. This is usually regional/city based as the gangs link themselves to local teams and clubs
   - Frustration – some fans can become very frustrated if their team is not doing well or if they feel that many of the official's decisions are going against them and this can manifest itself in disorderly behaviour
   - Displays of masculinity – this is a particularly male characteristic often displayed by young males (4 marks)

4 Award up to 4 marks for:
   - A large crowd can lead to safety concerns/there will be increased safety costs/additional stewards have to be provided/rival supporters have to be separated both on the way to and from the ground so additional police costs will be added/there is more likelihood of pitch invasions (4 marks).

Page 68

1 **d)** (1 mark)

2 **c)** (1 mark)

3 Award up to 3 marks for the following:
   - a state of complete physical/mental/and social well-being/and not merely the absence of disease or infirmity (3 marks)

4 Award up to 3 marks for the following:
   - So you do not suffer discomfort/being able to bend sufficiently to tie up shoelaces/put socks on/reach up to get a book from a shelf (3 marks).

Page 70

1 d) (1 mark)
2 c) (1 mark)
3 a) (1 mark)
4 Award up to 2 marks for each category as follows:
Physical factors:
- possible increased chance of cancer
- increased chance of heart disease and heart attacks
- increased chance of diabetes
- increased chance of high cholesterol

Mental factors:
- generally causes ill health
- increased chance of depression
- loss of confidence

Social factors:
- a possible inability to socialise
- a possible inability to leave home – this is quite common in extreme cases (6 marks).

Page 74

1 b) (1 mark)
2 Award up to 3 marks for the following:
- the intake of food/considered in relation to the body's dietary needs/good nutrition is an adequate/well-balanced diet/combined with regular physical activity (3 marks)
3 Award 1 mark for each correct response:
   a) endurance athletes
   b) gymnasts, jockeys and any performers in weight category linked activities
4 To maintain fluid levels/to avoid dehydration/heat exhaustion/to stop the body weakening to the point where it will stop functioning (2 marks).

Notes

Quick quizzes at www.hoddereducation.co.uk/myrevisionnotes